D0106720

HOW TO SURVIVE A HORROR MOVIE

BY SETH GRAHAME-SMITH

QUIRK BOOKS
PHILADELPHIA

Copyright © 2007, 2019 by Quirk Productions, Inc.

Library of Congress Cataloging in Publication Number: 2006939743

ISBN: 978-1-68369-146-4

Printed in China

Typeset in Univers LT Std, Bembo Std, Portmanteau, and Frontage Condensed
Designed by Andie Reid
Illustrations by Chris King
Production management by John J. McGurk

Quirk Books
215 Church Street
Philadelphia, PA 19106
quirkbooks.com

The publishers and author (especially the author) hereby disclaim any liability from any injury that may result from the use, proper or improper, of the information contained in this book. We do not guarantee that this information is complete, safe, or wholly accurate, nor should it be considered a substitute for your good judgment and common sense.

Nothing in this book should be construed or interpreted as an excuse to infringe on the rights of other persons or to violate criminal statutes. We urge you to obey all laws and respect all rights, including the property rights, of others.

CONTENTS

AN APOLOGY FROM WES CRAVEN

There's something I've been meaning get off my chest. Something that's been eating away at my conscience for decades now. And I'll admit, it's not easy to write without getting a little choked up . . .

. . . I'm sorry.

I'm sorry to the countless people whose lives I've cut short. The characters who've become unwilling sacrifices to my art: The buxom babysitters. The doubting cops. The overbearing parents and well-intentioned boyfriends. Teens with their whole lives ahead of them. Decent, hardworking adults. All sent to an early grave in the name of box-office gold.

Some made my job a little trickier—valiantly struggling to make it to the end credits. Others did everything but cut their own throats—running upstairs when they should've run out of the house; falling asleep when their lives depended on staying awake.

I'd be lying if I said I hadn't taken pleasure in dreaming up ways to kill them. Disemboweling them. Beheading them. Burning them, shooting them, and crushing them in garage doors. I've tortured young girls in *Last House on the Left*. Picked off an entire family one by one in *The Hills Have Eyes*. Created a child-murdering monster with the power to kill people in their dreams.

I've built a career on the blood of innocents, and I guess the guilt's finally caught up with me.

Sure, I've tried to make amends before. Tried to give my characters a fighting chance. *New Nightmare* was the first step toward self-aware horror movie characters. *Scream* went a step further. For the first time, we had people who knew they were in a horror movie. Even better, they were armed with knowledge of the rules.

And yet they died.

No matter what I do, no matter how much of a head start I give them, it seems my characters always end up on the wrong end of a long knife. And while I'm happy that somebody's finally written a guide to helping them survive, I wonder how much good it'll really do.

Death finds a way.

—*Foreword to the 2007 edition*

INTRODUCTION

I've always had a special place in my heart for horror movie characters. You have to feel sorry for the poor bastards. Of all the film genres they might have found themselves in—romantic comedies, costume dramas, inspiring biopics—these unlucky chumps were spawned in that darkest and most desolate tract of cinematic real estate: the opening moments of a horror movie.

Whether it's the perky camp counselor, the overconfident scientist, or the security guard who leaves his post to check on "that weird noise," the odds of survival are not good for these pitiful wretches. Like the thousands of baby sea turtles who hatch from their leathery eggs and crawl toward the sea only to be snatched up by waiting predators before they even had a chance to live, precious few horror movie characters survive to see the end credits.

Before I was lucky enough to make horror movies of my own, I spent my formative years sitting in carpeted basements, lights off, watching these films on VHS. My friends and I screamed ourselves hoarse—not just because we were scared, but at the sheer stupidity on display. The poor choices being made. The obvious death traps being walked into. The sex being sexed.

Yet, as stupid and helpless as the victims in these stories were, I felt for them. Yes, I loved watching them get hacked to pieces. Yes, I laughed at their gruesome demises. Yes, I laughed harder when they died naked. But a little part of me—the part deep, deep down that still had the capacity to care for others—wanted to help them.

And so I wrote this book as a tribute to these most pathetic of creatures, in hopes that I might succeed in two noble pursuits: 1) helping even *one* person meet the horror movie odds, and 2) avoid being evicted from my apartment for back rent.

Of course, that was back in 2007. I was young and naïve. Though much of the advice I offered then remains valid, the Terrorverse has invented new ways to inflict bloody death on its citizens . . . and on *you*, should you ever find yourself trapped in a horror movie. (Perhaps you're in one already; chapter one will help you figure that out.) This updated edition draws from plenty of new and noteworthy horror movies to keep your survival skills up to date. It features new tactics, new artwork, and an updated appendix of must-see horror flicks. I've learned a few things in the ensuing years. A few more skills to dodge the kills.

Now come with me if you want to live . . .

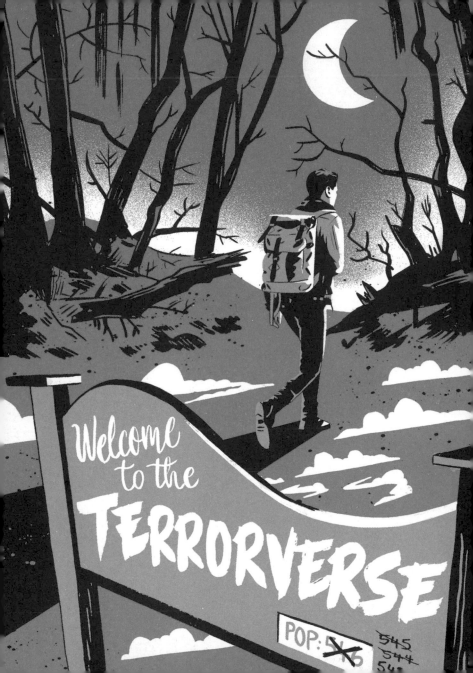

CHAPTER I

WELCOME TO THE TERRORVERSE

DR. LOOMIS
Death has come to your little town,
Sheriff. Now you can either ignore
it, or you can help me to stop it.

—HALLOWEEN (1978)

Those of us who've become trapped in a horror movie have a choice: We can either line up with the other cattle and march into the slaughterhouse, or we can fight back. Yes, it's a long way to the final credits. No, the odds aren't in our favor. But that's no excuse to lie down and let the filmmakers have their way with us. Choose to learn the new rules. Choose to use them in your favor.

Choose life.

HOW DO I KNOW IF I'M IN A HORROR MOVIE?

Horror movie characters aren't killed by machete-wielding monsters or reincarnated psychopaths—they're killed by ignorance. Ignorance of the mortal danger they're in. Of the butcher lurking in every shadow. Of the new rules.

Ignorance of the fact that they're in a horror movie.

How do you know if you've been sucked into the Terrorverse? Sometimes the signs are unmistakable. For instance, if you're a teenaged babysitter caring for a mute toddler in a remote Maine cabin during a once-in-a-century blizzard while an escaped killer (bearing a strange resemblance to the handicapped boy you and your friends bullied off an embankment and left for dead all those years ago) roams the woods, you're *probably* in a horror movie.

But unless you've landed in the sloppiest of direct-to-video hack jobs, the clichés are going to be more subtle, your screenwriter more inventive, and your survival less likely.

1 DETERMINE HOW YOU CAME TO OWN THIS BOOK.

In movies, things rarely happen without a reason. Therefore, the simple fact that you're holding a book called *How to Survive a Horror Movie* means someone's probably trying to tell you something. Think hard: How did you end up holding this book?

"I'm just browsing in a bookstore." There's still a chance it's just coincidence. Be warned, though—if you take this thing to the counter and buy it, your chances of being in a horror movie go through the roof.

"I ordered it online." This is not good. Computers can be a gateway to unspeakable evil. Perhaps you were merely enticed by the gorgeous cover and incredibly reasonable price.

"Someone gave it to me as a gift." Yikes. Getting a book called *How to Survive a Horror Movie* as a gift? That's like your spouse signing you up for life insurance "which you'll probably never even need."

"I found it in the woods." There's only one genre that would allow clumsy, contrived screenwriting like that. Proceed directly to chapter 2, "Slasher Survival School," page 45.

2 TAKE A LOOK AROUND. The environment should offer some clues. If you're on a crowded city street in broad daylight, you're probably safe (for now). But if you're anywhere remote—the woods, an old house, an abandoned mental institution in the middle of a blackout—then yes, your chances of being in a horror movie are much higher. How the location looks and sounds can be helpful, too:

Does everything look slightly grainy? This could indicate that you're being shot on film. Or that you're developing cataracts. Either way, not good.

Is it poorly lit? Is everything bathed in bright blue light even though it's supposed to be nighttime? Are there shadowy corners that you should be able to see into but can't?

What is the set decoration like? Can you see children's sidewalk chalk drawings that should've washed away ages ago? Is everything suddenly covered in cobwebs or rust? Is there a thin layer of smoke on the ground for no reason?

Do you hear strange sounds? Do strange *chi-chi-chi . . . ah-ah-ah* or metal-on-metal noises seem to come out of nowhere? Does music crescendo every time you open a door?

Are you speaking Japanese? According to the laws of early twenty-first century cinema, anyone speaking Japanese is in a horror movie.

Are you on surveillance footage? If everything around you is in black-and-white and looks like low-resolution video shot from a fixed camera mounted on a pole or in the corner of the ceiling, you're likely part of some "found footage" that documented something horrible.

If the answer to any of these questions is "affirmative," then we have to consider the possibility that you've become trapped in a horror movie.

3 TAKE A LOOK AT YOURSELF. Are you or any of your companions wearing a varsity letter jacket? Is there an achingly attractive yet sexually paralyzed female in your midst? Do all of your "friends" look suspiciously like cast members from *Riverdale* or *Supergirl*? (If so, your chances of meeting an untimely end have just increased by a factor of 10.)

Determine if you fit any of the classic horror movie character stereotypes:

A "The Nice Guy with the Monosyllabic First Name"

B "The Slutty Goth Chick"

C "The Virginal Cop's/Priest's/Richest Man in Town's Daughter"

D "The Nerd" (or "Nebbish Jew")

E "The Congenial Fat Guy" (or "Deputy")

 A

 B

 C

 D

 E

 F

 G

 H

F "The Sex-Crazed A-Hole" (or "Italian")

G "The Black Guy Who Buys It 20 Minutes In"

H "The Black Guy's Girlfriend Who Buys It 24 Minutes In"

If these bear an uncanny resemblance to you (or your companions), you're almost certainly in a horror movie. But before we panic, let's confirm the diagnosis.

4 CONDUCT THE M.A.D. TEST. M.A.D. stands for "Motivation And Dialogue," and it is one of the quickest, most accurate ways of confirming the presence of the Terrorverse.

Motivation. If you (or your friends) feel strangely compelled to do any of the following, you're definitely in a horror movie:

† Dig up a coffin to "make sure" something's really dead.

† Harass a hobo or intellectually disabled child.

† Play with a Ouija board or read from a dusty old book.

† Have sex in that house where that guy killed his whole family.

† Carve a crucifix into your face with a rusty screwdriver.

Dialogue. Ask each of your companions: "What time is it?" If they answer with the following, you're in deep trouble:

† The A-Hole/Italian: "Time for some pussy, that's what freakin' time it is."

† The Black Guy's Girlfriend: "Oh hell no."

† The Nerd/Nebbish Jew: "Wow, I didn't even think you knew my name."

† The Slutty Goth: "I'm your ex, not your Rol-ex."

† The Fat Guy: "Mmpph hrff rurrph." (Mouth full of lasagna.)

5 **CHECK THE CALENDAR.** There are only three months in the horror movie year: July, October, and December.

In July, teens are off from school—free to drink, wear bikinis, attend summer camp, and take each other's virginity at will. October is, of course, the unholiest of months—when long-dead serial killers, ghosts, witches, and all manner of beast return to the world of the living to seek revenge. And December is reserved for Christmas killing sprees, evil Santas, possessed stepfathers, gremlins, and snow-bound caretakers.

If the nearest calendar reads "May," you can relax a little. However, if every Friday falls on the 13th, forget the month. You're toast.

6 **CHECK YOUR WATCH.** The horror movie day is still 24 hours long, but 21 of those hours are at night. If it's almost always dark, all signs point to a horror movie. Ditto if the moon is always full. But even more telling than the lopsided night/day ratios are the huge gaps in your personal space-time continuum.

If you find yourself asking, "How did I get here?" again and again, it's probably because an editor has lopped out all the boring bits of your daily existence: walking from point A to point B, camping on the sofa for a Netflix binge, and taking showers (unless you're a girl with spectacular boobs).

ARE YOU IN A SEQUEL?

You're probably thinking, "Who cares? Isn't it bad enough that I'm in a horror movie?" Well, yes—but knowing whether you're in the first, second, or seventeenth installment is important. The later you appear in the series, the higher your chances of survival. With every subsequent sequel, the writing gets sloppier, the killer's methods more predicable, and the danger zones more pronounced.

EXAMPLE: Let's say you're offered a job as a camp counselor. You go online, do a Google search on the camp's name, and get 370,000 articles about the murders that have occurred there every summer for the last 20 years. Result? You spend the summer flipping burgers and keeping your limbs.

But how can you be sure? Here are a few sequel warning signs:

△ You're attending a nondescript college in an unidentified state, and your friends keep saying things like, "Can you believe we're in college now?"

△ You have shaky, black-and-white flashbacks of someone else's unhappy childhood.

△ Jamie Lee Curtis is your mother.

△ You're in space.

△ You're in 3-D.

△ You have the oddest feeling that you're only here for the money.

HOW DO I KNOW WHAT TYPE OF HORROR MOVIE I'M IN?

You've used all of the diagnostic tools outlined in the last chapter, and you've arrived at the terrifying yet undeniable conclusion: Somehow, you've managed to become trapped in a horror movie. Now what? Just skip ahead a few pages to find the magic cure that'll fix everything? Don't waste your time—it doesn't exist. Saying "I'm in a horror movie" is kind of like saying "I'm in Europe." Sure, you've narrowed it down to a continent, but what language should you use to order dinner? What side of the road should you drive on? Can you take off your top at the beach?

There are many subgenres (and sub-subgenres) in the horror movie universe—each requiring different survival skills. They can be broken down like this:

Slashers. Blade-wielding psychopaths (human and supernatural).

Evil places and things. An evil vehicle, a killer doll, or a haunted house.

The undead. Ghosts, zombies, vampires, and the reanimated.

Monsters. Werewolves, aliens, and weird things that you can't get a good look at.

Satanic. Demons, witches, curses, and the devil.

This book contains the tactics to help you survive each and every one of these subgenres. Now it's time to pinpoint your location.

1 **GATHER CLUES FROM YOUR MOVIE'S SETTING.** You've already scanned your surroundings for the usual horror movie suspects. Now it's time to take a closer look. Your location can speak volumes about the movie's subgenre, assuming you know how to read the tea leaves:

> **An isolated/dilapidated house.** If you're a young female alone in the house, all signs point to a slasher. If you're joined by friends or relatives, it's a haunted house. If the windows and doors are boarded up, there are about 7,000 zombies outside waiting to feast on your brains.

> **A summer camp.** You're in a slasher movie.

> **Deep space.** You're either in a really well-made alien flick or a nauseatingly bad, late-in-the-series slasher flick.

> **The Midwestern United States.** Hard to tell. This could be anything from a non-supernatural slasher to an evil vehicle rampage. However, if your friend finds a meteorite in the woods, you should probably shoot him in the face and burn his body. Just to be safe.

> **A constantly overcast city.** Urban horror movies are almost always Satanic in nature. Curses and demons should be high on your list of concerns.

> **Western Europe.** You're in a werewolf movie.

> **Eastern Europe.** You're in a vampire movie.

2 **DETERMINE YOUR MOVIE'S BUDGET.** Subgenres often break down along budget lines, so it can be very helpful to get a fix on how deep the producers' pockets are. Three things to observe:

Location. Are you in the city or the suburbs? (It's much more expensive to shoot a movie in a city.) Do you live in a luxury home or a run-down one-bedroom? (Set construction is costly.) How much freedom do you have to visit different places? (The more you move around, the more sets have to be built or location fees paid.)

Look. Does the lighting seem natural, or are you distracted by how flat and harsh it is? (Could the production afford a talented cinematographer?) How nicely is everything decorated? If you open desk drawers, are there supplies inside, or are they empty? (How big was the art department's budget?)

Licensing. Do you hear any popular songs or watch any real movies or TV shows as you go about your day? (If so, the producers had to pay through the nose for the rights, suggesting a higher budget.)

If everything points to a cash-strapped production, you're probably in a low- or even micro-budgeted horror flick—the most common kind. If you're not exactly sure where your movie falls, it's likely that the filmmakers are working with a modest budget. And if you feel as if no expense has been spared, it's possible that you're in the seldom-seen big-budget horror movie. So how does this help you figure out the subgenre?

Low or micro budget. The photography isn't particularly eye-catching, there aren't more than a few major settings, and you're nowhere near a city. Possible subgenres: slashers, the undead, evil places and things.

Modest budget. Day looks like day, night looks like night, and you're able to visit well-populated public places. Perhaps you live in a charming, richly decorated farmhouse or luxury apartment. Possible subgenres: the undead, fangs, satanic.

Big budget. Really? If you are in a horror flick, it's almost certainly alien or satanic in nature. But it's more likely that you've made the common mistake of misdiagnosing a "psychological thriller" as a horror movie. If so, heed this advice: If you're looking for your child, he/she probably never existed. Also: your husband did it.

3 DETERMINE YOUR MOVIE'S TIME PERIOD. The overwhelming majority of horror movies exist in the present, mainly because they're made for teenagers, and the easiest way to scare teenagers is to show them other teenagers—who look and sound just like them—getting hacked to pieces, and because it's way, way, way cheaper to film in the present. But if you happen to find yourself wearing pantaloons or snoozing in a hyper-sleep pod, those subgenres become easier to sniff out:

The past. Consider the possibility that you're merely in a flash-back sequence—the one where the old lady hangs herself, thus making the house evil, blah, blah, blah. But if you're really stuck in the salted-pork era (specifically the eighteenth or nineteenth centuries) you're probably in a mummy or vampire movie—the only subgenres that dare to break the unwritten rule against making period horror flicks.

The future. Another rarity in the Terrorverse, a futuristic setting almost always means you're in an alien movie (although in a few cases, some overly ambitious slashers have made their way to the final frontier).

4 LOOK FOR DEAD GIVEAWAYS. Sometimes it takes careful deduction to figure out a movie's subgenre. But sometimes, a clue is so obvious that it eliminates the need for further analysis. A few examples:

† Your friend uses SPF one billion sun block at the beach. Subgenre: vampires.

† Slices of bread start screaming when you put them in the toaster. Subgenre: haunted house.

† Your husband seems distant lately—plus, he tries to order "brains" every time you go to a restaurant. Subgenre: zombie.

† A cat jumps out of every door, cabinet, window, oven, washing machine, jar, or tube of toothpaste you open. Subgenre: slasher.

† Bibles burst into flames if they're brought within reach of your child. Subgenre: the Devil.

C·R·A·V·E·N·
(COVER, RECON, ARSENAL, VEHICLE, ESCAPE, NORTH)

The time for analysis is over. You've been sucked into the Terrorverse, and as much as you may feel like crying or making skid marks in your tighty-whiteys, you'd better pull yourself together—and right soon. Because if you don't, the boogeyman's really going to give you something to cry about (assuming he lets you keep your eyes). Your situation requires immediate action, and the C.R.A.V.E.N. method was developed for just such an emergency. It's a kind of "stop, drop, and roll" for

KNOW YOUR HARBINGERS
OF IMPENDING DOOM:
THE DUAL CITIZEN

A dual citizen is a special breed of character found only in horror films. He or she is someone (usually an elderly man) who exists somewhere between the Terrorverse and the real world. Dual citizens always function in the same way: give the audience some neatly bundled back-story and force the protagonist to make a choice—either heed the warning and turn back, or ignore it and forge ahead. Inevitably, our hero always chooses option number two (otherwise, we wouldn't have much of a movie). But if your goal is survival, you'd be well advised to get the hell out of Dodge when some old codger tells you to, narrative structure be damned.

Here are three of the most common dual citizens to be on the look-out for:

△ The gas station attendant, who lives just down the road from the evil town and tells you not to go there, even though he seems relatively unaffected by the evil. (Why hasn't he moved away or called the cops in all these years?)

△ The local barfly who tells you a story beginning with "It was a night just like tonight . . ."

△ The homeless guy who grabs your arm after you toss a nickel in his cup, stares into your eyes, and says something prophetic, like, "If you're trapped in the house of hell, follow the right path to freedom." Of course, this advice eventually saves your life at the end of the movie, when you're confronted with two doors while escaping the serial killer's basement.

```
                        HERO
     One door on the left, one on the . . .
     right?

               (puts it together)
     Right path! "Follow the right path
     to freedom!" God, what clever
     screenwriting!
```

Still, you'd have been better off identifying him as a dual citizen and not entering the house of hell in the first place.

horror movie victims—a way to stay alive long enough to summon your courage and get out of immediate danger. So take a deep breath, stick to the letters, and come with me if you want to live . . .

TAKE COVER. Running around in a panic is the fastest way to end up with a machete in your back. What you need right now is a temporary headquarters—a place to wipe the sweat from your brow, take a pull off the old asthma inhaler, and formulate your plan. Some of the best places to do that:

> **Good ol' everyday houses.** Though not ideal fortresses, the average two-story house is almost always the closest option. If you're already in one, great. If not, run into the first one you see (if there's a family inside, even better—they'll call the cops, and horror villains tend to scatter when the cops arrive). Go to the highest floor, check all the closets, look under the beds, and use whatever you can to barricade the doors and windows.

> **Water towers.** If your movie takes place in a small Midwestern town, this might very well be the tallest structure around. If you can get to the top, you'll have a highly defensible (there's only that one long ladder to worry about) perch with a 360-degree bird's-eye view of the battlefield. Even better, the available water supply will allow you to stay longer if you have to.

> **Churches.** While the power of Christ won't stop all forms of evil (zombies are notorious agnostics), it'll slow down most demons, supernatural slashers, or vampires that happen to be on your trail. Even better, churches tend to have fewer exits to cover and plenty of pews to use for blockades. Lead-lined stained glass windows are tough to break through, and many churches have spires or bell towers that serve as great vantage points.

A word of warning: "Overbarricading" is a common horror movie mistake. People get so focused on trying to keep anything from getting in, that they forget to leave themselves a way out. For example, locking yourself in a bank vault might stop the killer in his tracks, but now what? Remember, the C.R.A.V.E.N. steps are strictly temporary—a way to stop the bleeding before the real surgery begins. Unless you're being chased by vampires, in which case you can just stay put till morning.

R **CONDUCT RECONNAISSANCE.** Now that you've had a moment to catch your breath, it's time to get an idea of where the enemy is and what he's up to. If you don't have the height of a church spire or water tower working for you, peek through the highest window in your hideout and take a look. Do you see the attacker(s)? Is he standing still or looking for a way in? Is he favoring one side of the hideout over another? If you're being pursued by a group, are there any areas where their ranks are thin? Is there an unoccupied vehicle or busy road in sight? All of this information will help you choose the most promising escape route.

If you see nothing, they're probably right behind you. No, wait! Don't turn around; just pretend you're still reading this page. Nice and cool . . . that's it. Now, on the count of three, cover your face with your arms and jump over the rail, out of the bell tower, or through the window. Either you jump or you die. Ready? One . . . two . . . just kidding, you're totally screwed.

A **GATHER AN ARSENAL.** You see a path to freedom—now all you have to do is fight your way down it. To do that, you'll need some kind of weapon. If you're barricaded in a house, look for a baseball bat, kitchen knife, or anything that kids aren't allowed to play with indoors. Even a can of oven cleaner is better than nothing. If you're holed up in a church, grab a heavy-duty candlestick or a collection plate, which can be thrown with deadly decapitating force. And if you're up on that water tower, get your hands on the nearest, um . . . actually, there aren't too many options with a water tower.

You really should've thought of that before you climbed up there.

V COMMANDEER A VEHICLE. You've summoned some courage, grabbed a weapon, and hopefully spotted a nearby unoccupied vehicle or busy road during your reconnaissance—now it's time to kick a little ass. In a burst of adrenaline-fueled speed, make a run for it, using your weapon to clobber, cut, or blind anything in your path. Your goal—your only goal—is to reach the nearest car or truck, get inside, and blow town as fast as inhumanly possible.

If you reach an unoccupied vehicle first, get in (don't bother smashing the window—they left the car unlocked), lock the doors, and pull down the driver's-side sun visor. The keys will simply drop into your lap. When you try to start the engine, it'll turn over again and again, but

don't worry—it'll kick in as soon as the attacker(s) reaches the car and pounds on the windows.

If you reach a busy road first, simply run into oncoming traffic and wave your arms wildly. Inevitably, an attractive member of the opposite sex will see you at the last second, skid, and smash into you. Yes, you've been seriously injured, but you've also just scored your love interest, and more importantly—your ride.

E MAKE YOUR ESCAPE. This is the easy part. Just bury the accelerator and don't look back. If you've just been picked up by that hot blonde, move close to her on that bench seat, stare into her eyes, and floor it.

N HEAD NORTH. In Terrorverse America, it's always better to be north of wherever you are. If you're in Maine, you'll soon reach the safety of (98 percent horror-free) Canada (ditto if you're in the creepy videotape-laden Pacific Northwest). If you're in the desolate Southwest, you'll be playing slots in Vegas before dawn. If you're on an alien-infested Pennsylvania farm, you'll be in Upstate New York—where few horror movies take place, since everyone forgets it's there. So put the car in "D," point the compass to "N," and get the "F" out of there.

THE SEVEN DEADLY HORROR MOVIE SINS

The Seven Deadly Sins date back to the earliest days of Christianity. They were devised as a way to keep followers from indulging their less attractive urges: lust, pride, wrath, gluttony, sloth, envy, and greed.

EJECTION SEAT #1:
THE GENRE SWITCHEROO

Should you find yourself in the clutches of certain death—fangs to your neck, knife to your throat—there are only four proven methods of making a last-minute escape, called Ejection Seats because of their drastic, last-resort nature.

EJECTION SEAT #1 is the Genre Switcheroo. The switcheroo works by doing something to confuse the killer (and the screenwriter) just long enough to get clear of the immediate kill zone. This is accomplished by doing something completely incongruous with the situation—something that leaves the audience asking, "Wait, is this really a horror movie?"

MOVE YOUR MOUTH OUT OF SYNC WITH YOUR DIALOGUE.
Demand to know where magic sword is. Use the words revenge or master in every sentence. Genre: martial arts.

FART. This should be easy, considering you're already moments away from making it in your pants. Genre: teen comedy.

SLIP YOUR ATTACKER THE TONGUE. Potentially gross depending on the type of killer you're dealing with, but quite effective. Genre: romance.

LIGHT A CIGARETTE AND CHASTISE YOUR ATTACKER IN ITALIAN.
Doesn't even have to be real Italian. Just use your hands a lot. Genre: artsy foreign film.

DELIVER A LONG, STOIC MONOLOGUE IN AN ENGLISH ACCENT.
About a lifetime of regret, unrequited love, and summers at the estate in Yorkshire. Genre: Merchant Ivory.

In Catholicism, these transgressions were (and still are) dealt with through confession and prayer. In the Church of Latter Day Horror Movies, however, there's a different set of seven deadly sins, and only one punishment . . .

1ST: **DOUBT.** There are two types of horror movie characters: those who believe your story and those who don't. And while believers are by no means safe, at least they've taken the first step down the long road toward survival. Doubters, however, can always count on being dead before the end credits.

> **"It was just a dream, honey."** No it wasn't. Come on, people. Your son, daughter, or best friend is having recurring dreams about getting brutally murdered night after night, and you're brushing it aside as what—indigestion? This is a horror movie. All nightmares are real. Treat them as such, or you'll be in one of your own before long.

> **"I've heard enough out of you!"** This line is almost always spoken by the father, cop, or combination thereof. The one who has every opportunity to step in and do something, but refuses to believe some punk's cockamamie story. And why should he? Sure, there have been brutal murders here for the last 12 consecutive summers, but he buried that psychopath in Old Man Hurley's tobacco field. Buried him with his own two hands. What—just because some dope-smoking kids saw something, he should drop everything and investigate?

> **"Those are just ghost stories our parents told us."** Yes, and they just happen to be true. If all the moms and dads in town have spent the last 17 years telling you not to go into the abandoned mannequin factory, here's an idea: Don't go into the abandoned mannequin factory.

2ND: MACHISMO.

The jock who thinks his football skills are enough to defeat the reincarnated serial killer. The redneck who intends to show that vampire how they do things in Texas. The soldier who's taken on aliens way scarier than this one. All tough, all dead. Remember, fellow males—in horror movies, testosterone might as well be cyanide.

"You want some of this?" You know the guy. The one who just can't take it anymore.

```
          MACHO GUY
What's your plan, huh? Sit and wait
for that . . . that thing to pick
us off one by one?

  (grabs the last shotgun shell)
No way, man! Not me.
```

He runs out into the open, yelling something like "C'mon, show your face, you pussy!" And . . . well, you know how that ends.

"You're perfectly safe as long as we're around." OK, stop me if you've heard this one before—the galaxy's toughest Marines go to this alien-infested planet, see?

"Shut up and make me some eggs before you get a black eye." The worst of all the machismo sinners is the abusive husband or boyfriend. If you mistreat a woman in a horror film, there's no book that can save you from your well-deserved, imminent, and audience-pleasing death.

3RD: INDEPENDENCE. Have you ever seen that documentary about wildebeests? The one where it's nothing but slow-motion footage of them getting torn apart by lions and crocodiles? Great, isn't it? Funny how the predators always seem to kill the animals that are on the outer edges of the herd. The ones who are either too slow or too stupid to draw strength from their numbers. This is not a coincidence.

> **"Screw you guys, I'm going home."** Actually, you're going about a third of the way home, at which point (after you've heard the second or third twig snap behind you) you decide that maybe this wasn't such a hot idea. But by then it's too late. As panic takes hold, you break into a jog . . . then a sprint, and then—oh, I won't spoil it for you.

> **"C'mon you guys, this isn't funny."** No, it sure isn't. Maybe you shouldn't have gotten distracted and wandered away from the others. Oh, and by the way, you have about four seconds to live.

> **"We can cover more ground if we split up."** You forgot to add "with blood" between "ground" and "if."

4TH: UGLINESS. Nobody said horror movies were fair. That goes double for people with acne, glasses, or cottage cheese in the seat. You see, in the "everybody's a teen model except the funny fat guy" world of horror movies, it's a sin to be anything less than drop-dead gorgeous. And while it's true that even the hottest of hotties sometimes gets disposed of, it's usually because he or she engages in one of the other deadly sins (especially number seven, page 38). It's rare that someone is killed for good looks alone. On the other hand, ugly people could put on body armor, lock themselves in a padded room buried beneath a mountain, and surround themselves with armed guards, and they'd still get wasted before the one-hour mark.

5TH: CURIOSITY. Have you ever been in a theater when the girl (in the movie) hears a strange noise and decides to see where it's coming from? Notice how everyone in the audience starts tensing up as she climbs the stairs? That's because they know one of the basic horror movie equations:

Investigation = mutilation.

Now that you are that character, remember that when you go to "check something out," the audience is getting tenser with every step. Especially if your dialogue includes any of the following lines:

"Is that you, Patches?" If "Patches" is your nickname for the naked man hiding in your closet with razorblades on his fingertips, then yes, it is.

"I wonder what that creepy old house looks like on the inside." Probably a lot like the inside of a creepy old house. One that you and your soon-to-be mutilated friends have no business setting foot in.

"Do you think it's dead?" No. Go ahead and poke it with a stick. We want to watch it grab your arm and bite half your face off.

6TH: IRRESPONSIBILITY. If you're supposed to be guarding the door, then guard the door. Don't wander off to take a leak. If you're supposed to be watching the kids, don't do bong hits with your headphones on. If you're supposed to wake your friend up at the first sign of a bad dream, don't fall asleep. How hard is that? In a horror movie, if you accept a task and fail to carry it out, either you or someone close to you is going to die.

10 PLACES TO NEVER, EVER, EVER GO UNDER ANY CIRCUMSTANCES

1. Rooms lit by a single hanging light bulb.

2. Rooms lit by nothing.

3. Any graveyard that isn't Arlington National Cemetery.

4. Summer camps whose annual counselor murder rate exceeds 10 percent.

5. Maine.

6. "The old _____."

7. Hotels/motels that aren't part of giant international chains.

8. Upstairs.

9. Downstairs.

10. Any log cabin anywhere on the face of the earth.

† "Aw, what's a little nap gonna hurt?" A lot.

† "Trust me, the kids are sound asleep." No, the kids are dead.

† "How come I always get the crappy jobs?" Because you're an idiot, and you're about to prove that fact by failing miserably at the simple task you were assigned.

7TH: **VEHICULAR SEX.** Everybody knows the old adage about sex in horror movies: Do it and die. Well, yes and no. While it's certainly advisable to keep it in your pants while visiting the Terrorverse, there are plenty of people who have sex and live to brag about it. That's because they copulate in the comfort of their own homes, or the privacy of a respectable massage parlor. Because they avoid the one kind of nasty that's guaranteed to result in death: vehicular sex. The kind counselors have when they steal the equipment van and drive into the woods. The kind the prom king and queen have in the school parking lot. In the real world, sex and cars make

great bedfellows. But in the horror world, when someone asks for a long, hard rod in their trunk, hand them the tire iron.

HOW TO SURVIVE A HORROR MOVIE HIGH SCHOOL

When you're in a horror movie, nothing's more dangerous than a building full of 14- to 18-year-olds. Not demons, not serial killers, not chemical weapons—nothing. And since you're a current guest of the Terrorverse, there's a very good chance that you are a high school student. At the very least, you have some kind of affiliation with the school—whether it's as a teacher, a parent, or recent alumnus. Therefore, it's crucial that you understand the many, many dangers of being in a place where the Freshman 15 refers to the number of murders per semester. Use them to your own benefit, or pass them on to friends and loved ones. Either way . . . welcome to Horror High.

1 **UN-CLIQUE YOURSELF.** When screenwriters craft their cliché-laden horror scripts, they might think, "Hey, what about a funny fat guy?" or "Hey, a pissy Goth chick would be perfect here." But they almost never think, "Hey, I need a totally nondescript character that's hard for my largely teenaged audience to categorize."

Bingo. Your goal is to be a human chunk of tofu—something that mixes well with everything but remains completely uninteresting (or unappetizing, your pick) on its own. This can be largely accomplished with a new dress code:

Clothing. For boys, the recommended uniform is a pair of well-fitting blue jeans, a white, grey, or black T-shirt (no slogans, band names, or logos), and low-cut sneakers. For girls, a plain knee-length skirt, unrevealing earth-tone top (preferably covered with a black cardigan), and ballet flats.

Hair. If you're a boy, go to the local big-name franchise hair salon and ask for the following: short (not messy) on top, round in the back, and number two on the sides. Decline any offers of hair gel, and lose the sideburns. Obviously, facial hair is out of the question. For girls, anything pulled back into a ponytail (no bangs) should do the trick.

Accessories. As a general rule, they should be avoided. But if you must, keep it simple: cheap watches (no throwbacks, calculators, or wide-bands), thin gold or silver necklaces (no religious symbols, lockets, or name plates), and simple earrings (girls only, and no hoops—only whores wear hoops).

2 MAKE FRIENDS WITH THE SHOP TEACHER. Even when the other teachers turn out to be aliens or vampires, you can count on the shop teacher's blue collar virtues to win the day. Plus, he has power tools.

3 DON'T USE YOUR LOCKER. In horror movies, there are only four things that can happen when you're caught standing at your locker, none of them good:

† You're harassed by the school bully. This sets off your need to teach him or her a lesson, leading you to the cornfield rave and, ultimately, your gruesome death.

† Your friend has a great idea—some childish prank that leads you to piss off someone you shouldn't have and, ultimately, your gruesome death.

† You find something creepy hanging inside, which sets off an ancient curse, leading you to become a living vessel for a long-dead demon and, ultimately, your gruesome death.

† You watch the new girl/boy walk down the hallway in slow motion. Next thing you know, you are on a quest to nail her or him, leading you to realize that he or she's actually a murderous psychopath and, ultimately, your gruesome death.

4 POLITELY DECLINE ALL AFTER-SCHOOL INVITATIONS. Just as nothing good can happen at a locker, no good can come from accepting an invitation to do anything after school in a horror movie:

† "Hey, you want to go keep me company while I babysit tonight?" No thanks, I'll take my chances juggling flaming razor-finned piranhas at my house. I figure it's safer.

| "Hey, I heard there's this huge party at . . ." Stop right there. That "huge party" will turn out to be three ugly guys and a bored girl drinking warm beer in the woods, each of whom will be eaten when they wander off to pee.

† "Oh my God, you should totally come camping with us." Oh my God, I totally shouldn't, 'cause you're so getting decapitated!

† "We're going to sneak into that boarded-up hotel tonight and read Latin from this book we found." Have fun. I'll be in Antarctica.

5 **AVOID SCHOOL FUNCTIONS LIKE THE PLAGUE.** Forget the Spring Social and the homecoming game. Your goal should be spending as little time with the students and faculty as possible. Every second you're in their sight (or even near the campus) is another second you're being exposed to danger.

6 **BE NICE TO EVERYBODY.** And that means everybody—from the biggest bullying dickhead to the lowliest headgear-wearing mouth-breather, no matter how you're treated in return. It has nothing to do with the Golden Rule, and everything to do with staying alive. Remember this: The Terrorverse abhors an asshole, and sooner or later, it finds a way of wiping them from existence.

SIGNS THAT YOU SHOULD STOP TEASING A FELLOW STUDENT IMMEDIATELY

△ All the doors in the room suddenly slam shut.

△ He or she gets a nose bleed.

△ You get a nose bleed.

△ He or she stares—unblinking—into the distance.

△ He or she says something even remotely like "I wouldn't do that if I were you . . ."

△ Wind starts blowing through his or her hair, even though you're indoors.

CHAPTER II

SLASHER SURVIVAL SCHOOL

MASKS, GLOVES, AND MOTELS

> NORMAN
> She just goes a little mad sometimes.
> We all go a little mad sometimes.
>
> —PSYCHO (1960)

Forget heart disease. Forget cancer. In the Terrorverse, slashers are the leading cause of death. More than half of us will perish under their knives, gloves, and axes—not because they're so clever, but because we (their prey) are usually stupid beyond comprehension. So put your clothes on, lock the door to your camp cabin, and let's get you out of this mess alive . . .

THE SLAUGHTERHOUSE FIVE: FIVE TYPES OF SLASHERS AND HOW TO DEFEAT THEM

slash·er—n.
One who slashes: a slasher of tires

The most common predator in the horror movie universe, slashers are named for their tendency to use sharp objects to violently kill or mutilate human prey.

Like a shark's, a slasher's beauty lies in its simplicity. It's the perfect killing machine—an engine of death. Every molecule—every action—is devoted to extermination. And just as there are hammerheads, great whites, and nurse sharks, slashers also come in different shapes and sizes. There are three species—the living, or *Slashus Vitalis* (serial killers; other psychopaths); the sort-of-living, or *S. Semianimis* (reincarnated mental patients); and the not-so-living, or *S. Mortalis* (dead child murderers). And each of those species can be further divided into five types—all requiring different skills to identify and defeat.

1 THE STRONG, SILENT TYPE

How to Identify Them: SSTs often wear masks and coveralls to hide their disfigured or decaying flesh and never, ever speak (either for psychological reasons or because their vocal chords have decomposed). Thanks to their freakishly large physiques, they can walk faster than humans can sprint. SSTs have no pain receptors, so they take being shot, stabbed, or dismembered in stride. Their weapons of choice are butcher knives and machetes, and their primary habitats are small towns and heavily wooded areas.

How to Defeat Them: Smarts. You can't outrun them, and you certainly can't take them on, but you can capitalize on their Achilles' heel: one-dimensional thinking. SSTs are single-minded creatures—they see only what's directly in front of them and think only about the victim at hand. This tunnel vision makes them extremely vulnerable to traps—especially those that use decoys (human or otherwise) to lure them in. And once you've got them where you want them? There are only two ways to permanently silence the silent: (1) Burn them until they're reduced to ash, mix that ash into wet cement, and use that cement to build a children's hospital; or (2) crush them in a hydraulic press, put the remains through a wood chipper three times, and feed the shreds to puppies.

2 THE GAMESMAN

How to Identify Them: Gamesmen aren't satisfied with old-fashioned murder—they need to make you endure the unthinkable: kill your best friend or mutilate your own body, for instance. They spend incredible amounts of time planning their schemes, which almost always begin by drugging and kidnapping their victims, waiting for them to wake up chained to something, and taunting them over an intercom. Next comes the "just to show you how serious I am" display of violence, followed by the "if you want to live, you're going to have to [insert complex/terrifying task here]." Naturally, the promise of earned freedom is always a lie. Their weapons of choice are overbuilt torture devices and surgical instruments, and their primary habitats are urban warehouse districts.

How to Defeat Them: Play dumb. Ask for an explanation every time you're given an order, no matter how basic it is. If you're told to cut off your own hand with a pocket knife, ask, "Which attachment do you suggest?" Or "Should I start with the fingers and work my way up, take it off at the wrist, or what?" The Gamesman gets his kicks by playing God. Stupid questions force him down to your level—the

last place he wants to be. If you're able to get him flustered enough, he might make that one mistake that allows you to escape. Or put a .45 in your skull. Either way, the joke's on him. Who's gonna play his stupid game now, huh?

③ THE INBRED HILLBILLY

How to Identify Them: In a horror movie, if your car breaks down in some bone-dry, long-forgotten town, anyone you encounter is either an inbred hillbilly or working in close association with one. Here's how it usually goes: You're forced to rely on the only tow truck driver in the entire county, who turns out to be a roper for the local inbred family of serial killers. Before long, you find yourself trapped in their clown-themed dungeon, where you're tortured, killed, buried, dug up, and eaten. InHills kill because of their backwash DNA and because, frankly, they've got nothing better to do. Their weapons of choice are farm tools, and their primary habitats are anywhere noninbred hillbillies are found.

How to Defeat Them: Out-crazy them. InHills love to intimidate victims with displays of their inbred insanity—drinking from a jar full of severed testicles, dressing the hairiest family member in a little girl's leotard, etc. But you've got one weapon they don't: a twenty-first-century worldview. Intimidate them right back with tales of modern-day horror, such as things you've witnessed in nightclub bathrooms or German porn clips you've seen on the Internet. If those don't make them vomit and drive you to the county line, nothing will.

④ THE WISECRACKER

How to Identify Them: They're highly intelligent and highly inventive, and their timing is impeccable. Unlike other slashers, wisecrackers embrace the world around them—pop culture in particular. While another slasher might simply decapitate you, a wisecracker would decapitate you, toss your head into the garbage can, and say, "Nothin' but neck." They also have a strange proclivity to rhyme for no reason. Wisecrackers can be particularly hard to defeat, since the audience is usually rooting for them. Sometimes wisecrackers are dressed for the part, attiring themselves like a clown or that guy in the cubicle next to yours who's always good for a quip. Their weapons of choice are razor blades and humorously repurposed objects, and their primary habitats are small towns and nightmares.

How to Defeat Them: Play to their insecurities. Ask them why they feel the need to make all those jokes. Is it because they never got enough attention growing up? Are they afraid no one will like them unless they're constantly entertaining? Could this be why they feel the need to kill teenagers? The same teens that made fun of them all those years ago? Don't they see that by killing, they're just feeding into a vicious cycle of isolationism? If that doesn't work, just keep repeating the four magic words: "I don't get it."

5 THE MAMA'S BOY

How to Identify Them: Poor mama's boy. So damaged. So unloved. If only mother had let him play with other boys, maybe his taxidermy hobby would've stopped at rodents. Maybe he could have been a real doctor—the kind that helps people, instead of the kind that, well . . . doesn't. But no. She just had to keep yelling. Even when she continued to bathe him at age 14, telling him how filthy his body was. Telling him what a sinner he was. Mama's boys (who can also be girls) have to kill mother again, and again, and again. But she never dies. Their weapons of choice are butcher knives, and their primary habitats are unrestricted.

How to Defeat Them: Get them laid. Seriously. If they're about to drive a blade through your chest, hold up your hands, ask them to "wait a sec," and invite them out for a night on the town. Chances are they'll

THE TOOLSHED ARSENAL

If you're looking for a weapon in the Terrorverse, you can't go wrong raiding the nearest toolshed (or garage). But choose wisely!

TAKE IT:

△ **CHAINSAW**—the horror movie defensive weapon of choice. Light and deadly.

△ **HATCHET**—not as good as a chainsaw, but handy for cracking skulls and severing spinal cords.

△ **SICKLE**—either long- or short-handled. Great for slicing bellies open.

△ **AWL**—penetrates foreheads and eyeballs with ease and fits nicely in your front pocket.

LEAVE IT:

△ **SHOVEL**—too heavy on one end. Plus, you're giving the screenwriter a "forced to dig your own grave" opportunity.

△ **RAKE**—what are you going to do, scratch them to death?

△ **SAW**—we don't have all night.

△ **SLEDGEHAMMER**—unless you're Mr. T, wielding something that heavy is next to impossible.

drop the knife and start sobbing on the spot, since it's the first time anyone's ever invited them anywhere. Take them club-hopping, act interested in their rambling stories about squirrel anatomy, and slip a hot guy some cash to flirt with them (whether a mama's boy is male or female, they want a guy—trust me). This strategy will save yourself as well as untold numbers of future victims.

HOW TO SURVIVE SUMMER VACATION

Ah, to be young in the summer. To wake up on a glorious July day, birds singing on your windowsill, a soft breeze rustling the leaves of the oak you've climbed a thousand times. The world is yours. Time is limitless.

Only it isn't. This isn't real life, it's a horror movie, where long summer days begin with singing birds and end with your throat getting slit in the woods. When you're a teen (or young adult) on summer vacation, every day is the last day of the rest of your life. That is, assuming you make the same mistakes that young horror movie characters always seem to make.

1 STAY AWAY FROM CABINS. Cabins are the bug zappers of the horror movie universe—a place where the more gullible of our species are weeded out in one gruesome instant. "Hey, a cabin. That looks like a nice place to spend some OH GOD MY INTESTINES ARE ON THE FLOOR!" And like the bugs that keep flying toward that pretty light, people who decide to spend their summers in a secluded, run-down cabin have learned nothing from history and are therefore doomed to repeat it. The rule is simple: If you enter a cabin—any cabin, anywhere in the world—you will be dead within 24 hours. Guaranteed.

2 DON'T GO TO SLEEPAWAY CAMP. What, pray tell, has more cabins than a sleepaway camp? "Sure, I'm in a horror movie, but I really don't see the problem with hanging around a bunch of cabins in the middle of the woods—a bunch of cabins run by teenagers who spend their time smoking dope and humping." Are you crazy? No institution has a higher per-capita murder rate. For example, a high school of 1,000 students can expect an average per-film loss of seven to eight students, or less than 1 percent. A sleepaway camp of 40 campers and counselors, however, can expect the same per-film losses. That's a murder rate of 20 percent! Any horror movie character who willingly attends one of these death camps is making the screenwriter's job so insanely easy, they should get shared credit.

3 DON'T TAKE A ROAD TRIP WITH YOUR FRIENDS. There are only three things that can happen when young people pile into a car:

> **Someone insists they know a great shortcut.** This leads them to an eerily quiet town that's not on any map. Suddenly, something goes wrong with the car (all horror movie vehicles have sensors that stop the engine when they detect a combination of evil and isolation). Stranded, they're "rescued" by someone who promptly butchers them, wraps the choice cuts of meat in plastic, and stores them in their roadside diner's walk-in freezer.

> **They run someone over.** Inevitably they decide to ditch the body and keep it a secret, and they spend the rest of the movie getting picked off like scabs.

> **They safely reach their destination.** Except the destination is a cabin in the middle of nowhere.

HOW TO CONVINCE THE SKEPTICAL LOCAL POLICE

Sadly, those sworn to protect and serve the horror universe have a hard time getting motivated. So enlisting their help takes some skill:

1. **REMAIN CALM.** Show even the slightest bit of excitability, and you'll be considered hysterical. Nothing you say will be believed.

2. **PROVIDE COMPELLING PHYSICAL EVIDENCE.** A bloody knife, soiled clothing, or—best of all—a severed body part.

3. **USE REVERSE PSYCHOLOGY.** "Ah, it's probably nothing. I mean, sure, I watched that big fella drag that boy off into the forest, but I'd hate to see you go out there on some wild goose chase."

4. **LIE.** If you want the sheriff to check something out, give him an incentive. Tell him that his wife was seen there partying with members of a biker gang—whatever it takes to get him on site.

4 **DON'T GO BACKPACKING OVERSEAS.** Until recently, Europe was a fairly safe place for students to blow off steam between semesters. With the exception of England (werewolves) and countries ending in *-ania* (vampires), the worst you might encounter were haunted castles that, to be honest, were more charming than scary. But with more horror films choosing Europe as their location, those colloquial haunts are fast becoming nightmarish bloodbaths. Today's backpackers have to be on the lookout for human traffickers, dog-killing psychopaths, even spell-casting preteens. Australia is also becoming increasingly dangerous for foreigners. There was a time when meeting a knife-wielding loner from the Outback was the prelude to a fish-out-of-water romantic comedy. These days, it's fatal.

But the most dangerous international destination for Western travelers is Japan. With so many horror flicks coming out of the land of the rising sun, it's best to treat the entire island as one gigantic cemetery. The only place you're safe is in the heart of Tokyo, which (so far) seems reserved for coming-of-age romances, street racing movies, and OH GOD a giant fire-breathing lizard!

5 **BORROW SUMMER ACTIVITIES FROM OTHER GENRES.** Sure, there are plenty of things you can't do on your horror vacation, but does that mean you're condemned to a summer of watching YouTube videos? Your break can actually be quite fulfilling, especially if you borrow a few activities from your favorite non-horror films:

> **Go on a life-affirming quest with some child stereotypes.** Perhaps you could follow an old treasure map or walk down the train tracks in hopes of seeing your first dead body. Just make sure your posse has at least one fat kid, one "bad" kid, and one sensitive intellectual with (1) recently divorced parents or (2) a recently deceased older brother.

Fall for the new neighbor boy or girl who dies in the second act.
You'll laugh. You'll cry. You'll still be alive for the funeral scene
at the end of the movie.

Save some land from a bunch of developers. Nothing stops urban
sprawl in its tracks like a few kids who still believe in a little thing
called "home."

WHAT TO DO IF YOU DID
SOMETHING LAST SUMMER

1. ASK YOURSELF, "WHAT DID I DO?" Last summer could have been ages ago. What? You're supposed to remember every little thing you did between June and August? Chances are it wasn't something innocuous. The filmmakers have to hang the entire premise of the movie on one thing—one action taken by you, the character. Things like that tend to stick out in the memory banks.

THINGS YOU DID LAST SUMMER THAT AREN'T MOVIE-WORTHY:

△ Cheat on your diet.

△ Sneak store-bought candy into a movie theater.

△ Have sex on the football field.

△ Pool hop.

△ Use illegal P2P file-sharing networks.

THINGS YOU DID LAST SUMMER THAT ARE MOVIE-WORTHY:

△ Cover up a manslaughter.

2. DETERMINE IF ANYONE KNOWS WHAT YOU DID. If you get a letter from someone claiming they know what you did, chances are someone knows. Likewise, if you had accomplices who also did what you did, it's likely that they know, too. It's recommended that you kill any accomplices as a means of reducing the number of people who know what you did.

3. IF SOMEONE KNOWS WHAT YOU DID, FESS UP. Admit to the crime, and do the time. Yes, being in a prison movie isn't roses, but it beats the hell out of being a victim in a horror movie.

HOW TO SURVIVE A
NIGHT OF BABYSITTING

In the real world, babysitting is a groovy way for young people to learn responsibility (and earn a little pocket money). In the Terrorverse, it's a plot device used to kill teenagers.

Babysitters are the juiciest of all slasher bait—more attractive than drunk gravediggers or horny campers. As we've learned, horror flicks (especially slashers) are made for teenaged ticket buyers, and teens can identify with the tensions of babysitting. You're away from home. You can't bail at the first sign of trouble. Devils and angels duke it out on your shoulders: "Don't get high tonight." "C'mon . . . invite him over—he's so cute!" And then what happens? The power goes out. You try the phone . . . nothing. Suddenly, you remember that news report. Something about a string of murders. Footsteps upstairs. Kids missing from their beds. And faster than you can say "closed casket," you join a long list of sliced-up sitters. Unless . . .

1 **KNOW WHEN TO SAY "NO."** If you have half a brain in your head,* the answer is always "no." In horror movies, babysitting is basically suicide at seven bucks an hour. It's a dangerous game, and to quote one of my favorite passages from the Book of Joshua (the supercomputer in *WarGames*, not the apostle), "The only way to win is not to play." And yet for many teenagers, the desire for extra mall cash is stronger than the will to live. Therefore, it's important that whippersnappers be able to distinguish the really, really dangerous babysitting jobs from the 100-percent-chance -of-getting-your-throat-sliced-open babysitting jobs. If the offer includes any of the following, turn it down. It's a guaranteed death sentence.

---

* Ironically, this is exactly what most horror movie babysitters end up with.

It's more than two blocks from home. Anything beyond shouting or sprinting distance is too far.

There's a storm in the forecast. Thunderstorms equal power or phone outages and opportunities for the director to use the old "lightning flash reveals the killer in the window" bit. Snowstorms equal broken-down vehicles and easily followed tracks.

One of the children is blind, deaf, or mute. It seems cruel, but remember: This isn't the real world. In horror movies, children with some kind of sensory deprivation or disability are often portrayed as creepy.

There's an escaped _____ on the loose. Any noun you can imagine in that blank space is reason enough to skip the gig, with the possible exception of "pony."

2 **MAKE YOUR EMPLOYERS SIGN A BABYSITTING RIDER.** A rider is a contract that specifies a list of perks. A smart sitter will craft one that ensures maximum survivability. Only work for employers who meet its terms. Some suggestions to pass along to your lawyers:

Power. Employer will provide a fully fueled backup generator that can be started without leaving the house or going into the basement.

Communication. If Babysitter attempts to contact Employer's cell phone at any time and gets no answer, Babysitter has the right to abandon the kids and run home.

Punctuality. If employer is more than sixty (60) seconds late for the agreed return time, Babysitter has the right to abandon the kids and run home.

Temptation. Employer will leave no unlabeled videos, alcoholic beverages, pornographic materials, or anything that might tempt Babysitter into committing lewd, unsavory, or potentially curse-invoking behavior anywhere in the home.

Security. Employer will provide doors and windows that can be securely locked from the inside, a professionally installed security system, and at least two (2) easily accessible, fully loaded firearms.

3 **BUILD A FORTRESS.** With no storms in the forecast, no escaped mental patients on the news, and your parents within shouting distance (and assuming your employer has met all the terms of your rider), the babysitting can begin. But before you even think about making the kids a snack, priority one is turning a small area of the house into an impregnable fortress. This "no in or out" zone usually includes the kitchen, living room, and at least one bathroom, and never encompasses more than one floor.

Start by closing (and, if possible, locking) all the doors on the edge of your perimeter and hanging little bells on the knobs. Confirm that all windows are closed, shut any drapes or blinds, and turn on every light within reach. Next, turn the TV on and tune it to a local station, in case there are any breaking reports of nearby murders, escapes, or storms. If the basement door falls within your perimeter, nail at least three big wooden planks across it. Finally, set the alarm, check the phone for a dial tone, and tether yourself to each child with a length of rope.

4 **DON'T DO ANYTHING EVEN REMOTELY IRRESPONSIBLE.** The minute you take your eyes off those kids—the minute you choose indulgence over vigilance—you're dead. Here's a rule of thumb: If you wouldn't do it in front of the parents, don't do it.

KNOW YOUR HARBINGERS
OF IMPENDING DOOM:
NUDITY

Or, more specifically, female nudity. We've already established that sexuality is a murder magnet in the Terrorverse, but experts estimate that this effect is 6.02×10^{23} times greater for female characters than for males. Scientists theorize that the exposed skin of a woman emits a high-frequency sound that only horror movie antagonists can hear; the strongest signal seems to come from the chest region. Unfortunately, one female character must expose that area of the body for the film to earn its R rating (violence and gore are, apparently, more acceptable for a young audience than the naked human form). Whatever the cause, every serial killer, supernatural monster, and alien creature knows that the female nude-sign indicates the presence of not only a potentially vulnerable victim, but possibly also a distracted, fumbling, addled male nearby—an irresistible two-for-one deal of death. Your best precaution: If you're male, make a quick exit the moment any female flesh is exposed. If you're female, dress in the ideal outfit for survival: baggy cargo pants, boots, and a parka over a ski jacket over two sweatshirts over two bras. Remain so garbed until the movie is over.

Some common babysitter pitfalls include:

† Inviting your boyfriend or girlfriend over.

† Raiding the liquor cabinet.

† Watching the parents' porn collection.

† Using the phone for endless personal, gossip-filled calls.

† Leaving the kids to entertain themselves.

5 NEVER, EVER, EVER ANSWER THE PHONE. Regardless of what the caller ID says, let it ring. If it's the parents, they'll leave a message. If it's one of your friends, you shouldn't be chatting with them anyway. But we both know it's not the parents or your friends. Why? Because this is a horror movie. And in a horror movie, it's always the killer, who is always calling from another part of the house. Your screenwriters are begging you to answer that phone. They need you to answer it, so their villain can send chills down your spine with some clever one-liner. All the more reason to let it go to voicemail.

6 CHECK YOUR CURIOSITY AT THE DOOR. What I really mean is stupidity. Check your stupidity at the door. Here are three situations you might face during a night of babysitting, each with the (soon to be dead) "curious" person's and the (might make it to the end credits) "incurious" person's response:

ONE OF THE WINDOWS IS RATTLING.

Curious: You decide to check it out, despite the fact that you swear you remember closing it.

Incurious: You set fire to the house, abandon the kids, and run home screaming.

THE HORROR
MOVIE SMARTPHONE

Do smartphones makes our lives better or worse? Future historians will decide. But in the Terrorverse, you can expect your phone to consistently fail when you need it most. Here's what you can count on from your phone in a horror movie:

△ **NO SIGNAL.** If you're lucky this will happen at the beginning of the movie, so you won't expect it to be of any use in critical moments.

△ **DEAD BATTERY.** And if you think you can find the right charging cable, let alone an outlet, forget it.

△ **CONDUIT TO EVIL.** As mentioned, killers love to phone their victims or, worse, FaceTime them. There go all your data minutes!

△ **BAIT.** Did you leave your phone somewhere? Don't go after it, or you'll end up being ambushed. True, a serial killer's probably flooding your Insta with gross selfies, but is that your biggest concern right now?

△ **HEY, IT'S WORKING!** Unfortunately, you're crouched behind a packing crate in an abandoned factory hiding from an axe murderer . . . and that's when someone decides to call you, and your loud, embarrassing Imagine Dragons ringtone will be the last thing you ever hear.

Your best bet? Toss the phone into a furnace and get on with the business of not being eviscerated. Besides, you have everything backed up to the cloud, right?

THE CHILDREN DISAPPEAR.
Curious: Panicked, you search every nook of the house while calling out their names.
Incurious: You continue reading your Bible and wait for them to turn up.

SOMEONE KNOCKS ON THE DOOR, ASKING TO USE THE PHONE TO REPORT AN ACCIDENT.
Curious: You open the door a crack to get a better look at the stranger.
Incurious: You empty a full clip through the door, reload, open it, and empty another clip into whomever or whatever is lying motionless on the front porch.

HOW TO STAY AWAKE FOR A WEEK

Staying awake and staying alive are often synonymous in horror movies. Perhaps your dreams have become the killing fields of a demonic slasher. Maybe you've been stranded on an alien-infested planet or cornered in a house that's surrounded on all sides by zombies. In any case, not an ideal time to hop the choo-choo to Sleepytown. And since there's no telling when the rescue party may arrive (or when it'll be safe to dream again), a horror movie survivor has to be able to push the outer limits of sleep deprivation. Believe it or not, the world record for going without sleep is held by a teenager named Randy Gardner. In 1964, he stayed awake for 264 straight hours—exactly 11 days. All you're required to do is a measly seven. And if you follow these steps, you might just make it.

1 **TRY TO JUMPSTART A MONTAGE.** What's the easiest way to stay awake for a week? Make it fly by in the span of a single upbeat song. Musical montages aren't common in the horror universe, but they aren't out of the question either. After all, this is still a movie—and in movies, it's possible to condense lots of events and time into a short series of illustrative shots, one dissolving into the next. Since these shots are rarely accompanied by dialogue, they're usually set to music—a song that'll boost sales of the soundtrack, for instance.

So how do you force the filmmakers into using one? Easy. There are two main categories of montage: the Prep and the Honeymoon. The Prep follows a character as he or she studies or trains for some nearly impossible task—usually a school test or sporting event.

The Honeymoon tracks a relationship through its early days—holding hands in the park, painting their first apartment (oh look, they're splashing paint on each other!), and so on.

Therefore, there are two main methods of jumpstarting a montage:

Start a new romance. Don't be picky. You're not choosing a life partner, just someone who'll stick with you through a Mariah Carey ballad.

Get in way over your head. If you've never thrown a punch before, sign up for a boxing match. If you're on the shallow end of the IQ pool, challenge a Nobel laureate to a battle of wits. In other words, totally screw yourself into spending the next five minutes of the movie in a series of gyms or libraries.

2 **BE PREPARED FOR SLEEP DEPRIVATION.** If your efforts to jumpstart a montage fall flat, you might just have to do this the hard way—by staying awake for seven days. And if that's the case, you'll need to know what to expect as the hours pass:

† Diminished problem-solving skills. You might want to schedule those Mensa exams for another week.

† Irritability. That's right, I said you're being a total dick. Now what are you gonna do about it?

† Diminished motor skills. Is it getting harder to turn the pages?

† Difficulty focusing your eyes. If you've waited too long to read this section, the words probably look blurry.

† Short-term memory loss. As you become more and more sleep deprived, you might experience as you become more and more sleep deprived, you might experience some memory loss.

† Paranoia. I'm watching you read this book. Right now, at this very second. I'm always watching. We're all watching.

† Hallucinations. In extreme cases of sleep deprivation, a person might become convinced that . . . hey . . . why is my hand that flying dog thing from *The Neverending Story*?

3 COMBINE STIMULANTS. When you're pulling an all-nighter during finals, you can get by on a cocktail of coffee, energy drinks, and diet pills. But that time-honored combo is only reliable up to about the 36-hour mark. Once you cross the two-day barrier, relying on mass quantities of caffeine and sugar just doesn't cut it. To make it to the finish line, you'll need to drop the sugar altogether—sure, it lights you up for a little while, but it also sends you plummeting into the depths of sleepiness afterward. You'll also need to strictly regulate your caffeine intake—taking small doses throughout the day and night (as opposed to a few gigantic doses, which also leads to sleepy crashes).

Then, you'll need to combine these artificial pick-me-ups with more natural forms of avoiding bedtime:

Temperature. You know that wonderful feeling when you snuggle under the warm covers on a cold winter's night? Well, it'll kill you. Keep as cool as possible, even if it means standing in the refrigerator or pouring ice cubes down your pants.

Light. This is especially important in the Terrorverse, where the vast majority of the day is shrouded in darkness. Try to remain in brightly lit areas at all times, and avoid windows like the plague. The goal is to throw off your body's internal clock.

Movement. Just as a rolling stone gathers no moss, a moving person gets no sleep.

Discomfort. Don't cut off your eyelids or anything (although that'd do the trick). Try the discomfort associated with "holding it in." Make sure to drink plenty of water to keep your kidneys busy, and don't worry—all that caffeine will take care of everything else.

4 **EAT RIGHT.** And eat often. Just as it's vital to regulate your caffeine intake, it's important to keep your metabolism even—as opposed to riding the three-meal roller coaster. Ever wonder why you get that food coma after a big meal? It's because your body is transferring its energy to digesting that big lump of take-out you shoveled past your gums. Instead, eat small, long-energy meals around the clock. Focus on foods that provide a steady stream of power, namely complex carbohydrates (pastas, grains) and proteins (meat).

5 **HIDE IN THE DELETED SCENES.** If you feel like you're not going to make it—if you can't go another day without grabbing some shut-eye, hide in the deleted scenes. After shooting, editors delete scenes that prove unnecessary—perhaps because they do nothing to

move the story forward, feature poor performances, or simply run too long. Therefore, you should try to spend all your time being as pointless, unconvincing, and long-winded as possible.

6 FORCE A TIME SKIP. In movies, time is mutable. This is because the audience (and the film editor) rely on certain cues that indicate that time has passed. Change the cues, and time must follow suit. It's an advanced technique that is similar to starting a montage, but involves more creative thinking on your part. Some ways to achieve this effect:

† Wear a second outfit underneath your clothes. Use a dimmer switch to fade the room into darkness, quickly whip off your outer clothing, and then bring up the lights to reveal that you're dressed differently than before. Start talking as if a day, or even a whole week, has passed.

† If your house lights don't have dimmer switches, achieve a similar result by walking into a room, closing the door, and then emerging wearing different clothing. Repeat several times a day. Comb your hair differently each time.

† Get a page-a-day desk calendar. Stare closely at it as you rip of the pages one by one and toss them to the floor.

† If it's a sunny day, employ a confederate to spray a window of your house with a garden hose while you're inside staring out said window. State how the forecast had called for "seven days of rain" before the sunny weather returned. Then signal for your friend to shut off the water.

† If all else fails, start talking about yesterday's events as if they happened a week ago. Then act as if they haven't happened yet. Then talk about an occasion that's months away—Christmas, the Fourth of July, someone's birthday—as if it is happening today. With any luck, the film editor will become so confused about the sequence of events that she'll just move you forward to the end of the movie.

EJECTION SEAT #2:
THE JARRINGLY GOOD DIALOGUE

Should you find yourself in the clutches of certain death—fangs to your neck, knife to your throat—there are only four proven methods of making a last-minute escape, methods called Ejection Seats because of their drastic, last-resort nature.

EJECTION SEAT #2 is the Jarringly Good Dialogue. The JGD works by delivering a line that's far too lyrical or thought-provoking for a horror movie. Delivering such a line temporarily paralyzes the killer as he awaits further instruction from the screenwriter, whose ego has shattered after realizing that they never could have written something that good. Don't worry—nobody's expecting you to pluck Shakespeare out of thin air. Simply memorize one of these classic movie lines and keep it handy for the occasion:

"Of all the gin joints, in all the towns, in all the world . . .
she walks into mine."—Casablanca

"Old age. It's the only disease, Mr. Thompson,
that you don't look forward to being cured of."—Citizen Kane

"A man who tells lies, like me, merely hides the truth. But a man
who tells half-lies has forgotten where he put it."
—Lawrence of Arabia

"Horror has a face . . . and you must make a friend of horror."
—Apocalypse Now

CHAPTER III

INANIMATE EVIL

MANMADE INSTRUMENTS OF DEATH

```
MR. HALLORANN
You know, some places are like
people. Some shine, and some don't.

—THE SHINING (1980)
```

Most of our horror movie enemies are people. Slashers, vampires, zombies, and ghosts all are or were human beings. Even aliens and demons fall under the sentient being umbrella. But sometimes evil has no flesh. Sometimes it lurks not in the hearts of men, but in bricks and mortar. Chrome and steel. Antique tea sets. Inanimate enemies can be even harder to defeat than their able-bodied counterparts. You ever try to stab a three-bedroom colonial?

Believe me, it's not very effective.

HOW TO SURVIVE A HAUNTED HOUSE

In the old days, spotting a haunted house was a piece of cake. It was always the creepy Victorian with the unmowed lawn and freakishly large weather vane.

But that was then. In the modern Terrorverse, it doesn't matter if the house is falling apart or brand-spanking new, sitting atop Graveyard Hill or shoehorned into an exclusive gated community. Any combination of wood, concrete, and paint can be haunted. And for that reason, every horror homeowner should know what to do in the event of a ghost or poltergeist infiltration.

Remember: In horror movies, you don't gut the interior . . . the interior guts you.

1 CONFIRM THAT THE HOUSE IS HAUNTED.
Just because your zip code is 00666 doesn't mean you have to run screaming every time a floorboard creaks. Even in the Terrorverse, sometimes a strange noise is just a strange noise. On the other hand, sometimes it's a portal to a dimension of unspeakable evil.

To help homeowners tell the difference, two professors at the University of Eastern West Berlin (Drs. Brenton Sabellico and Eric Dugre) came up with their famous questionaire of the 10 Questions in 1964. Homeowners simply circle "Yes" or "No" after each question. If you answer "Yes" to three or more of these questions, we can conclude beyond any reasonable doubt that your house is haunted. Proceed to step 2 immediately.

THE 10 QUESTIONS

1. Do the faucets or showerheads bleed?   YES NO

....

2. Did the previous owners die as the result of a murder
   or suicide?   YES NO

....

3. Does furniture rearrange itself when you aren't looking?   YES NO

....

4. When you reach into the refrigerator, does your arm
   appear in another part of the house?   YES NO

....

5. Are there Civil War–era children playing in your attic?   YES NO

....

6. Does the house issue verbal or written warnings?   YES NO

....

7. Does the temperature suddenly plummet if you discuss
   remodeling?   YES NO

....

8. Do you feel more compelled to murder your family
   with an ax than usual?   YES NO

....

9. Are Native Americans constantly showing up to ask,
   "What happened to our cemetery?"   YES NO

....

10. Does the house contain any candelabras?   YES NO

....

2 ONCE YOU'VE CONFIRMED THE HAUNTING, LEAVE IMMEDIATELY.

There are two things you can't change in this world: a husband who lets the dishes pile up, and a haunted house. Both lead to nothing but frustration, fear, and, eventually, a gruesome death. If the 10 Questions come back positive for a haunting, get out. Don't pack up your things. Don't go for one last dip in the half-finished swimming pool. Run. Now.

3 ESCAPE ON AN X AXIS. If the Y axis measures something's vertical position, the X axis refers to its horizontal location. Now, this next point is very important:

Inside a haunted house, moving along the Y axis gets you killed.

If you're upstairs, do not go downstairs. If you're downstairs, do not go upstairs. Zigzag to your heart's content. Run around in circles. Whatever you do, maintain altitude. If you're on the second floor of a haunted house, crash through the nearest window. In fact, do the same thing if you're on the first floor. Yes, you'll probably get hurt. But cuts and bruises are better than having your soul sucked into purgatory with a bunch of dead people who lost their road map to Hell.

4 BE ON THE ALERT FOR COMMON HAUNTED HOUSE TRICKERY. You're eager to leave, but the house is just as eager to keep you around. Once it realizes you're trying to escape, it'll throw every trick in the bag at you.

The Endless Hallway. A classic. As you run toward that door to salvation, the hallway becomes longer . . . longer . . . impossibly long. Countermeasure: A burst of willpower is usually all it takes. But closing your eyes is an easier way of neutralizing the effect. Just stick your arms out, and feel your way down the hall.

The Zero-Gravity Room. You're dragged up the walls by some unseen force. Countermeasure: Easy. Sing Lionel Richie's "Dancing on the Ceiling" and act like you're having the time of your life. The house will vomit you out the front door.

Coffin Whack-a-Mole. All the coffins from the graveyard you (so rudely) built a house on start shooting through the floor. Countermeasure: Inappropriately grope the corpses. The house will vomit you out the front door.

The Reappearance of a Dead Friend/Child. As the house becomes desperate, it'll deliver some low blows. The most common is recreating someone who's recently died. "Mommy . . . where are you going? Why are you leaving me?" Countermeasure: If the house isn't pulling any punches, neither should you. Address the "person" in front of you as the house, and tell it something that will set it off. Something like: "You should know . . . I've been sleeping in a condo."

5 **DO NOT GO BACK INSIDE.** If you do manage to escape, don't look back. Keep running, no matter how many screams echo through the night and no matter how fun it might be to watch the house fold itself into a point of light no bigger than the period at the end of this sentence. Never, ever go back.

Unless it's for the dog.

WHAT TO DO WHEN AN EVIL VEHICLE WANTS YOU DEAD

The engine purrs, the doors lock, and Martha and the Vandellas' "Nowhere to Run" crackles over the radio. Just one little problem:

You haven't put the key in the ignition yet.

Cars and trucks are dangerous enough when someone's behind the wheel. When they start driving themselves? You might as well give Helen Keller a bazooka. In horror movies, once a vehicle becomes self-aware, there's only one thing it wants in its tank: blood. And until it's topped off (or sent back to the scrap heap of Hell), no one's safe. It won't break down, it won't misjudge a corner, and it definitely won't stop until everything in its path is road kill.

1 **IF YOU'RE IN THE VEHICLE, GET THE HELL OUT.** Cars and trucks can take punishment that would turn the human body into a bag of liquefied organs. Knowing this, the naughty ones often go Kamikaze, locking their prey inside and kissing a telephone pole at 90 miles an hour. Result? They get towed, you get buried.

If you're trapped inside a stationary evil vehicle, use anything you can to smash a window, climb out, and run. However, in the more likely event that the vehicle is moving, you're going to have to smash that window and jump for it before you become a permanent part of the steering column.

1 Apply the emergency brake. This might slow you down slightly (assuming the vehicle lets you engage the brake). If it's a manual transmission, you can try downshifting. But don't get your hopes up—most evil vehicles don't accept user input.

2 Jump perpendicular to the direction of the vehicle. Don't fling yourself under the rear tires, which would be counterproductive to your survival.

3 Aim for a forgiving landing site. Grass, sand, and tall brush are more preferable to pavement. Anything's preferable to a tree trunk.

4 Tuck and roll. As you fly through the air, pull your arms, legs, and head close to your chest. When you hit the ground, roll to dissipate the energy of your impact.

2 IF YOU'RE NOT IN THE VEHICLE, SCAN YOUR IMMEDIATE SURROUNDINGS.

You may be safe from spilling your brains all over the dash, but you can still be rammed, crushed, and run over. Take a quick look around—is there anything to shelter you from an attack?

THINGS THAT WILL PROVIDE PROTECTION FROM EVIL VEHICLES:

High ground. This might come in the form of a steep, gravel-covered hill, cliff, or rooftop—preferably one that's attached to a sturdy building.

Deep water. An 18-wheeler can do a lot of things, but swimming isn't one of them. If there's a lake, river, or ocean anywhere in sight, get wet.

EJECTION SEAT #3:
THE AWKWARD PRODUCT PLACEMENT

Should you find yourself in the clutches of certain death—fangs to your neck, knife to your throat—there are only four proven methods of making a last-minute escape, methods called Ejection Seats because of their drastic, last-resort nature.

EJECTION SEAT #3 is the Awkward Product Placement. What's the hero's favorite beer? Chances are, the brand that's just written a big check to the producers. Product placement is a much-loved means of padding a movie's budget, but the filmmakers usually take great care to keep it subtle. After all, you can't have your characters making obvious pitches.

If you find yourself cornered by a horror villain, try buying precious time with the clumsiest, cheesiest advertisement you can imagine. Doing so will confuse your attacker, and maybe—just maybe—allow you to escape.

> YOU
> You can crush my skull, but you can't
> crush my thirst . . .
> > (turn to imaginary camera)
> The way a refreshing Blue Bird Cola can!

> YOU
> There's no need to clean out my
> bowels with that machete! Just
> use . . .
> > (turn to imaginary camera)
> Gut Grease natural laxative-the brand
> trusted by more astronauts!

                    YOU
I may be crying, but it's not because
of soapy eyes! That's because I
use . . .
        (turn to imaginary camera)
Pupil Soft Shampoo, from the good
people at McMillan's!

Industrial buildings. Is there an office tower nearby? A shopping mall? School? Concrete is your friend.

The woods. In most horror movies, the last thing you want to do is run into the woods. But if the trees are dense enough, they'll stop most vehicles in their tracks. Now all you have to worry about are the 3,000 other things coming to kill you.

THINGS THAT WON'T PROVIDE PROTECTION FROM EVIL VEHICLES:

Single-family homes. Anything with a wooden frame can be breached by an evil vehicle.

Chain-link fencing. In movies, chain-link fencing might as well be rice paper with a bull's-eye on it.

Utility poles and radio towers. They certainly qualify as high ground, but they're too flimsy—especially if your pursuer is an evil truck or a construction vehicle.

Other vehicles. This is a horror movie, remember? Any car you enter is guaranteed to have a faulty engine.

1 COUNTERATTACK. Hopefully, once you've found a safe place, the vehicle will get frustrated and drive off to its next victim. But if it keeps coming, you have no choice but to engage—and quickly. Waiting it out is not an option. For starters, the evil vehicle can wait a lot longer than you can. Also, it can summon other vehicles to its aid at any minute. And if that happens, there's not an office tower in the world that will protect you. There are only two surefire ways to bring down an evil vehicle:

Shred the tires. Depending on just how evil it actually is, a vehicle might have the ability to repair itself. But that ability is almost always limited to its metal portions. Therefore, evil cars and trucks have an Achilles heel—four of them, actually. Find a way to pop the tires, and your enemy will be struggling to back out of the driveway.

Torch it. Fire: the great horror movie equalizer. Flames wreak havoc on everything from wiring to upholstery, and once the flames reach the gas tank . . .

2 MAKE SURE IT'S DEAD.

When the evil engine finally gives out, you need to move quickly to make sure it stays dead for good. First, crush it. This will require speed, since the car might be trying to repair itself. If you don't have access to a junkyard compactor, drag it to the bottom of a hill and roll a boulder onto it. Or take it to the woods and cut a sequoia down to fall on it. Or park it on some train tracks. Be as creative as you want, but work fast.

Once you've smashed it to bits, gather up all the metal scraps and take them to a steel mill. Melt the scraps into liquid and have it cast into several small ingots. Take the ingots out to sea (a deep lake will do) and throw them in the water one by one, letting great distances pass between each ingot's watery grave, just to be on the safe side.

3 MAKE SURE IT NEVER HAPPENS AGAIN.

If you want to permanently keep your car in neutral (paranormally speaking), consider the following:

Don't give your car a pet name. Not only is it dangerous, it's downright pathetic. Stop buffing the hood with a diaper and go find out what it feels like to kiss a girl.

Buy foreign. I'm just as red, white, and blue as the next guy, but facts are facts—97 percent of all the evil vehicles featured in horror movies rolled out of the Motor City.

Go two-wheeling. Motorcycles, scooters, and dirt bikes can't become self-steering killers, due to the fact that they'd fall over once they stopped moving. An evil scooter only deserves to be laughed at.

HOW TO DEFEAT A KILLER DOLL

Sometimes deadly things come in small packages.

The world's worst pickup line, but a superb reminder for anyone trapped in a horror movie. Dolls have always been vessels for evil, whether it's the wooden dummy who's sick of having someone's hand up its bad place, the marionette that cuts its own strings, or the child's toy that's through having its buttons pushed. It doesn't matter if they're powered by dead serial killers, brought to life by ancient curses, or just plain evil—they have to be taken seriously, no matter how cute their little scaled-down overalls are.

1 **KICK THE CRAP OUT OF IT.** Even if you're 12 years old, you're probably five to seven times larger than your attacker. Why are you running away from something that could be imprisoned with Legos? Before you resort to the fancy tactics that follow, crack your knuckles, step in the ring, and take your yarn-haired nemesis for a stroll down Pain Lane. Rip its limbs off. Pull its stuffing out. Hold it by the feet

and whack its head against the sidewalk. There's a reason dolls have to rely on stealth and trickery to kill—they're not very strong. You, on the other hand, have the gift of brute force.

2 MAKE THE PUPPETEERS MISERABLE. You lost a fistfight to a doll? Well . . . OK, try some other tactics (but I don't recommend you go around telling people).

The filmmakers have painted themselves in a bit of a corner. A slasher or werewolf can be played by a guy in a suit, but a tiny doll forces them to rely on special effects—namely animatronics controlled by off-screen puppeteers. That means the bad guy has to be connected to a bunch of wires, and those wires need to be hidden. This severely limits the little bugger's movements. (The doll might be computer generated if your movie's budget allows, but CGI has its own limitations.) If

10 THINGS TO NEVER, EVER, EVER PUT IN A CHILD'S ROOM

1. **ANY REPRESENTATION OF A CLOWN.** Whether it's stuffed, painted, or otherwise.

2. **INDOOR PLAY TENTS.** Anything that obstructs the child's view of the room (or your view of the child) is a no-no.

3. **WINDOWS.** In horror movies, windows are things that kids get snatched out of by vampires and scary trees.

4. **DOORS.** Does this sound familiar? You hear the children screaming and run to their room, only to have the door slammed in your face by whatever ghost is about to eat their soul.

5. **ONE OF THOSE TOY MONKEYS THAT BANG CYMBALS TOGETHER.** These serve absolutely no purpose other than coming to life when something scary is about to happen.

6. **FRAMED PHOTOGRAPHS OF DEAD RELATIVES.** Or photographs of any dead people, for that matter. Even Abe Lincoln or Mother Teresa.

7. **OUIJA BOARDS.** Come on.

8. **ANY CRUCIFIX FEATURING AN OPEN-EYED JESUS.** Directors love cutting to "creepy-pupils Jesus" to build dramatic tension. Don't hand them an invitation.

9. **BEDS WITH MORE THAN FOUR INCHES BETWEEN THE BOX SPRING AND FLOOR.** The bed's legs should also be chained to the floor, and younger kids should sleep wearing a climbing harness tethered to a secured steel cable (in case of an attempted spiritual abduction).

10. **CLOSETS.** What are you, crazy? Nail the door shut and buy a dresser.

you're still running away (from a doll, mind you), these tactics will make it next to impossible for the tiny terror to give chase:

Get some fresh air. The killer doll's natural habitat is indoors, because it's easiest for the filmmakers to hide its gadgetry by cutting holes in sofas or building false floors. City streets and grassy fields present a whole truckload of problems for the effects department.

Go for a dip. The thought of getting wet sends chills down the artificial spines of killer dolls (and their puppeteers). With all those electronic components, swimming is suicide. If the doll is CGI, all the better; rendering an animated figure that's moving through water is a nightmare.

Pick the doll up. Yes, I know it's trying to chase you down and stab you, but hear me out. If you pick it up and hold it over your head, there will be nowhere to hide the wires, and thus no way for the doll to move. If the doll is CGI, the animators will balk at having to match its movements to yours, so give it a good shake and watch the image turn into a wire frame.

3 EMPLOY PROVEN ANTI-DOLL TECHNOLOGY. Being trapped in a killer doll movie is like winning the horror lottery. Let's face it—you have to be an idiot to get knocked off in one. Imagine the last thing you ever saw was a Cabbage Patch Kid standing over you with a knife. Imagine dying with that deep sense of shame.

> LIL' RANDY
> (licks knife)
> You're my best pal!

```
                    YOU
                  (dying)
   Please  don't  .  .  .  tell
   anyone  .  .  .  about  this  .  .  .
```

Luckily, you don't have to, because there are a few easily accessible weapons that no killer doll can survive:

Fire. Propane torches, furnaces, or cigarette lighters—any source will do. Your attacker is made of polyester stuffing and cheap plastic. He'll burn up faster than a Death Valley match factory.

Dogs. Killer dolls are terrified of dogs, probably because dogs love killer dolls. Namely, shaking them around, pulling their insides out, and eating their plastic buttons. And while dogs can be killed in certain horror movies, they're invincible in schlock-tastic killer-doll flicks.

Toddlers. Of all the doll's enemies, none is more feared than the common human toddler. Falling into the hands of a toddler is a fate worse than death, for it means suffering through an endless parade of tea parties, nap times, and dress-ups. And there's not a damn thing they can do about it, since no horror movie would ever let them kill the kid off.

HOW TO TELL IF AN OBJECT IS EVIL

Some inanimate objects are always bad: classic American cars (see page 77), intricately decorated boxes that may or may not open portals to Hell, and anything that gives its owner godlike powers. There's the family heirloom. The haunted computer. The demonically possessed cell phone. Hell, a website or even the whole Internet can be deadly (in addition to being a huge time suck).

> SATAN
> (into phone)
> Can you fear me now? Good.

But what about objects that don't fall under the "automatically evil" umbrella? Apply this checklist.

1 ARE NAZIS LOOKING FOR THIS OBJECT? If Der Führer wants it, it can't be good.

2 DETERMINE THE COUNTRY OR REGION OF ORIGIN. "You can take the item out of the evil, but you can't take the evil out of the item. Some parts of the horror globe (and galaxy) are particularly good at churning out dangerous artifacts and wicked trinkets. If your object's "Made in . . . " label ends with any of the following places, exercise extreme caution:

Egypt. According to Hollywood, every last pebble in the Nile Valley is a gateway to some ancient evil. So remember, "If it comes from a tomb, it leads to doom."

Sub-Saharan Africa. It's widely accepted that all African villages have demons that spend their time possessing young local girls. Therefore, any hand-crafted souvenirs (especially tribal masks) from that continent are likely carrying some residual evil.

The southwestern United States and Central Mexico. Any arrowheads, gold charms, or wood carvings you find in these regions are usually vessels for Indian or Aztec curses.

The Caribbean. In the eyes of Hollywood screenwriters, everything in the Caribbean is tainted with Voodoo.

Outer space. Objects from space are universally bad for horror movie humans. They're either carrying (1) space flu, (2) alien eggs/parasites, or (3) flesh-eating hairballs.

3 DETERMINE HOW IT CAME INTO YOUR POSSESSION. If any of these sound familiar, the object is almost certainly evil:

You unearthed it. Here's a cardinal horror movie rule: Anything you cover with dirt becomes evil. Whether you're an archeologist or gardener, objects found buried in the earth should be left there, no matter if they're one or 1,000,000 years old.

You bought it at a charming antique shop. Oops . . . all antiques are evil. Even worse, they come with a no-returns policy. (If you run back to the store to return it, you'll invariably discover that the store burned down 10 years ago. Ahhhhhhhh!!!!)

You found it next to a smoking crater. As a rule, any object found in the vicinity of a smoking crater should not be touched.

It was handed to you by a pale, sweaty priest who mumbled something about "seeing the face of the beast," then died. Ouch. You'd better pray he was high on LSD.

You stole it. You're toast. In horror movies, anything you take from its rightful owner comes with a 100-percent-cursed guarantee.

4 USE THE DOG TEST. Canines are more than bed hogs and volunteer vacuum cleaners—they're evil detectors. Their reaction will tell you what level of evil you're dealing with:

A **Spot takes no interest in the object.** The object is not evil. Feel free to display it on your mantle. Give Spot a rawhide for his troubles.

B **Spot barks at the object.** The object may be inhabited by a friendly ghost . . . or a bridge over which the armies of Hell will march into our world. Dispose of it immediately.

C **Spot pees on the floor and runs away.** The object is evil. Dispose of it immediately. Don't forget to clean your floor.

D **Spot drops dead on the spot.** Run screaming from your home and never return. Make no attempt to contact family members. Start a new life restoring boats in a small seaside town in Mexico.

5 CHECK FOR TELLTALE "EVIL OBJECT" FEATURES. Such as:

Unnecessary faces. Evil objects are often decorated with faces that serve no purpose other than being scary. Door knockers.

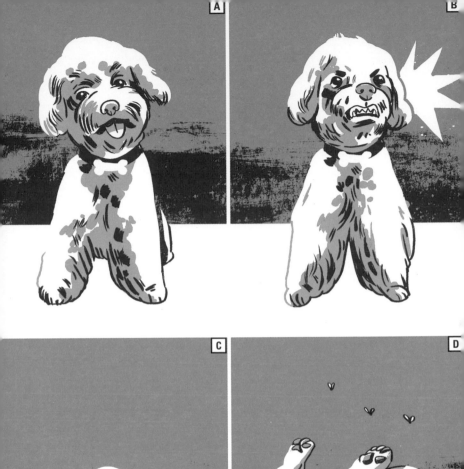

Banisters. Canes. If it's something the director can show in close-up to build tension, it's probably evil.

An overly complex, puzzle-like locking mechanism. Why the ridiculously overengineered locks? The longer it takes for something to open after the key is turned, the more suspense.

Words from a nonexistent language. How do you know if the language is nonexistent? Easy. If you can't read it, it doesn't exist.

Human skin. Anything that's covered in human skin (other than humans) is always evil.

An ominous name. The Necronomicon, The Lament Configuration, www.icleanmyteethusingyoursoul.evil—do these sound like things that anyone should mess with?

6 PROPERLY DISPOSE OF THE EVIL OBJECT. Once you've determined that an object is evil, don't go tossing it off a bridge for some other unlucky schlub to find—make sure it disappears for good:

† If the object is paper or wood, burn it to ash, mix the ashes with equal parts holy water, and use the resulting paste to paint a portrait of a smiling Jesus.

† If the object is metal, melt it down and turn it into a pair of crutches for a wounded veteran.

† If the object is plastic, douse in nail polish remover, light on fire, and use the resulting ash to paint a portrait of a smiling Jesus.

† If the object is stone, break it up into small pieces, and use those pieces as slingshot ammo to hold back the Nazis from step 1.

KNOW YOUR HARBINGERS
OF IMPENDING DOOM:
LIGHT

In the Terrorverse, light is usually your friend. It cuts through the menacing night, chases away the shadows where creatures lurk, and blinds night-vision equipped serial killers. But there are times when light is the last thing you want to see. Especially when it's coming from something (or somewhere) it shouldn't:

ANYTHING THAT ISN'T A BULB OR FLAME. There are some things—wood, metal, briefcases, stone—that aren't supposed to give off light. If they do, don't stare in slack-jawed fascination. Run.

KEYHOLES. If there's a powerful beam of light shooting through a keyhole, you can bet there's something very, very nasty on the other side of the door.

EYES. Light only radiates from the pupils of evil creatures, and it usually signals an imminent attack.

MOUTHS. If light is pouring from your mouth, you're about to be torn to shreds from the inside out and transported to another dimension—probably a bad one.

NOWHERE. The worst place light can come from is nowhere. Only the most powerful creatures are capable of self-illumination—namely demons and false gods. For dramatic effect, they'll backlight themselves to constantly appear in silhouette.

CHAPTER IV

CRYPT-OGRAPHY

GHOSTS, ZOMBIES, AND THE REANIMATED

PETER
My granddad was a priest in Trinidad.
He used to tell us, "When there's no
more room in hell, the dead will walk
the earth."

—DAWN OF THE DEAD (1978)

Dead people. Greedy sons of bitches. They had their time to exist, and now that it's over, do they float peacefully into the next plane of consciousness? No. They want more. An equal stake in our world. And until they get it, they'll rattle as many chains, terrorize as many children, and surround as many shopping malls as they can.

HOW TO SURVIVE
A CEMETERY

In the real world, people go to cemeteries after they die. In the Terrorverse, people go to cemeteries moments before they die. Boneyards are the hubs of just about every horror subgenre because cemeteries stir the creepiest nooks of our imagination. They're the place where our comfy little lives end and the long winter of death begins. And sooner or later, screenwriters will steer you to one. If you're any kind of horror movie survivalist, you'll run at the first sign of an epitaph. However, if the plot has made it impossible to avoid carrying a shovel through the gates, don't just gallop in, or you might end up staying far longer than you planned.

1 **KNOW WHEN IT'S TOO DANGEROUS TO ENTER.** Common sense dictates that it's always too dangerous to enter a cemetery if you're in a horror movie. That goes double if the answer to any of the following questions is "yes":

Did this land ever belong to Native Americans? You're in a movie, so the signs should be laughably obvious—a tattered teepee or nearby casino, for example.

Are ravens sitting on the old iron entrance gate? Trick question! If the answer is "yes," then there's obviously an old iron entrance gate, which is the real sign that you shouldn't proceed.

Is there a layer of smoke or mist over the ground? This would obstruct your ability to see things crawling out of the earth and make it more likely that you'd trip while trying to escape.

Is there fresh dirt next to any of the headstones? This one doesn't need any explanation.

Are there stone angels on any of the graves or crypts? Too tempting for the director. Stone angels will open their eyes and watch you walk by, which always means something bad is about to happen.

2 TEST THE SOIL'S REGENERATIVE PROPERTIES. All cemetery dirt has at least some regenerative ability. The question is, does it take years or minutes to work its magic?

On your way to the graveyard, stop at the market and pick up a fresh fish with its head still on. Before you venture too far into the cemetery, bury the fish a little below the surface. Wait five minutes, and then exhume it. Interpret the results as follows:

The fish is still dead. Marvelous. Proceed with caution.

The fish is wriggling ever so slightly. A discouraging sign. Anything you bury won't stay buried for long. Anything you dig up will be at least partially alive.

The fish is biting you. Not only is the soil extremely fast-acting (i.e., anything you exhume is going to be at full-strength), but it's also soured (i.e., anything you bury that isn't already evil will become so).

The fish bursts into flames. Hmmm. This is probably really, really bad. Run away.

3 DRIVE IN. Get that 4x4 as close to the burial site as possible before you step out—even if it means toppling a few headstones. And

when you're on foot, avoid walking over graves. Not because it's disrespectful, but because you're practically begging a zombie to thrust its hand through the soil and grab your ankle.

4 AVOID CRYPTS AND MAUSOLEUMS. If your mission leads you to the entrance of a crypt or mausoleum, know that you're staring down into of the darkest corners in the Terrorverse. A walled (often underground) tomb with a locking door is a favorite daytime hang-out for vampires (for tips on what to do if you encounter one, see page 114). Crypts should never be entered at night. Even during the day, it's safer to knock them down and sift through the rubble with shotguns at the ready.

5 ADHERE TO STRICT BURIAL GUIDELINES. If you're lucky enough to reach the burial site in one piece, don't go any farther until you've reviewed these rules:

Never bury someone alive. When's the last time you watched a movie where someone was successfully buried alive? They always escape, and they always come looking for you.

Never bury or exhume the bad guy. If your goal is to dig up the bad guy and make sure he's still dead, guess what? He's not. If your goal is to bury the bad guy because you're sure he's finally dead, guess what?

Never bury your child. Nothing's more painful than losing a child, except losing a child, having that child turn into a zombie, and having to kill that zombie child with your bare hands.

Always place a lightning rod next to the gravesite before you dig. Otherwise, the thunderstorm that kicks up the minute you start digging will result in a lightning strike that brings the bad guy back to life.

Don't stand in the hole when you open the coffin lid. As soon as you pry the lid off, the creature's going to spring up like a jack-in-the-box and eat your face.

6 SHOOT FIRST, NEVER BOTHER ASKING QUESTIONS. If something moves, shoot it. Either you've just dropped a zombie that was headed toward the smell of your tasty brains, or you've killed an innocent old lady laying a wreath on her husband's grave. Either way, give yourself a pat on the back. You did the right thing. Bury her, burn the wreath, and sleep well knowing it's better to be wrong than dead.

7 HAVE AN EXIT STRATEGY. You should always know what your next move is in case the creature leaps out of the coffin or the zombies close in. If you were smart enough to drive to the burial site, get back in the vehicle and lock the doors. As always, the engine will fail to start until at least one window is smashed by your attacker(s). When the vehicle starts, point the headlights at the nearest fence and crash through.

Remember: Surviving a cemetery is like surviving a war. And who'd go to war without an exit strategy?

THE GOOD, THE BAD, AND THE DEADLY: KNOW YOUR GHOSTS

Poltergeists. Specters. Free-floating, full-torso, vaporous apparitions. The real phantom menaces. Ghosts come in all kinds of exciting shapes and flavors. Some are merely nuisances, some are faithful companions, and others have the will (and the way) to drag a person out of this world. As a horror movie survivalist, you'll need to be able to tell the difference—and that starts with a lesson in the six ghost archetypes.

1 THE BUDDY. These are often the ghosts of children, and they spend their time trying to befriend living children. Buddies know they're dead. In fact, after a brief postfuneral depression, they learn to see their new ethereal status as a plus—using it to score living friends by performing ghostly tricks for their amusement. Buddy ghosts can also be recently deceased parents who feel compelled to see their kids grow up, or benevolent spirits that take a liking to the new family that moves in.

> **Sample Dialogue:** "If you need help with your Sunday school homework, I have a few connections!"

> **Danger Level:** Low. If your kids are going to hang out with dead people, these are the dead people you want them hanging out with.

> **How to Deal with Them:** Treat them as you would any other deceased friend or family member. If you're lucky enough to get one from an interesting historical period, the stories they tell

EJECTION SEAT #4:
THE COST-PROHIBITIVE LOCATION

Should you find yourself in the clutches of certain death—fangs to your neck, knife to your throat—there are only four proven methods of making a last-minute escape, methods called Ejection Seats because of their drastic, last-resort nature.

EJECTION SEAT #4 is the Cost-Prohibitive Location. Most horror movies are made on shoestring budgets, which is why they usually take place in inexpensive locations—the woods, a house, etc. The astute horror movie survivalist can take advantage of this. If you're being chased by a chainsaw-wielding killer, retreat to a location that the filmmakers (and thus, your attacker) can't afford to follow you to—somewhere requiring stratospheric location fees, hundreds of extras, and logistical headaches:

> **MANSIONS.** Shooting at a mansion is pretty easy from a logistics standpoint, as long as the filmmakers fork over the $25,000 a day that some homeowners charge for the privilege.

> **AIRPORT TERMINALS.** Shooting at a working airport is both expensive and time consuming, due to strict security guidelines, safety regulations, and ever-present noise.

> **MALLS.** Shooting in a store means dealing with managers. Shooting in a mall means dealing with the managers of all the stores. That is, unless filmmakers shut the whole place down, which few horror movies' budgets can afford. Then the mall must be filled with make-believe shoppers.

MUSEUMS. Filmmakers will have a hell of a time insuring burly union guys lugging lights and cables next to priceless works of art.

SPORTING EVENTS. Step one, pay the stadium. Step two, hire athletes to take the field. Step three, hire at least one seating section full of fans. Step four, declare bankruptcy.

CONCERTS. Filmmakers have to rent a venue, pay a band, dress the stage with all the necessary concert sound and lighting gear, and then fill the place with hundreds (if not thousands) of screaming extras—all of which cost big bucks.

LAW OFFICES. By the time the crew sets foot in the location, the producers will have so many contract restrictions, they won't be able to roll a foot of film without incurring some kind of financial penalty.

can be fascinating. They're also great for spying on the neighbors and deterring theft.

2 THE PEST.
Moving your furniture around. Locking you out of the house when you get the newspaper. Popping out of the drain when you're showering. Pests are the inmates who've been given the keys to the asylum. The class clowns who've been granted immunity from detention. They couldn't be happier to be dead. It's probably what they dreamt of their whole life. That's because now their immature pranks have the added benefit of being 100 percent consequence free.

> **Sample Dialogue:** "Yes! I have power over space and time, and I've decided to use that power to hide your underwear!"

> **Danger Level:** Low. They're annoying, but not interested in causing humans physical harm.

> **How to Deal with Them:** Like any pest, you can't give them the satisfaction of getting angry. Just ignore them. Don't laugh at their antics, and don't get angry at their childishness. Pretty soon, they'll get sick of playing a tough room and move somewhere else. Unless you're really something to look at in the shower.

3 THE CHARITY CASE.
These are ghosts who shook off their mortal coil without taking care of some important unfinished business. Business that they've decided to make your problem.

> **Sample Dialogue:** "Help me count every grain of sand on Waikiki Beach, so that I might have peace at last."

Danger Level: Moderate. If you cooperate with the errand, they'll be friendly. But if you fail (or blow them off), they've been known to exact revenge.

How to Deal with Them: Get it over with. If you have to deliver a message to his widow in Alaska, just go.

4 THE ATTENTION WHORE. They moan incessantly. Hover at the end of your bed. Write "get out" in the fog on your bathroom mirror. Day after day. Night after chain-rattling night. They just can't bear the thought of anyone else getting on with life—especially in "their" house.

Sample Dialogue: "Booooo! Aren't you scared? Oh God I'm so lonely."

Danger Level: Moderate. They're usually just crying out for attention. But in some cases, they go too far and harm the living, intentionally or not.

How to Deal with Them: They keep telling you to get out, but we all know that's the last thing they really want. Who would they have to haunt if you left? Invite the ghost to a sit-down, and make it clear that you'd like to be friends—but only if the moaning and chain rattling stop.

5 THE UNAWARE. Poor bastards. They have no idea. Just walking around like their flight landed safely. They'll even carry on with their daily routines. Sleeping next to their spouse. Driving their cab. Wondering why everyone seems so distant.

KNOW YOUR HARBINGERS
OF IMPENDING DOOM:
VISIBLE BREATH

When ghosts get angry, we get chilly. It's elemental horror movie science. Ghosts are slightly out of phase with our reality; they inhabit more than one plane of existence at a time. And because they're straddling two channels, they act as a sort of valve for energy to flow back and forth between them and us. The angrier a ghost gets, the more energy (heat) it robs from our plane. So when a room's temperature suddenly drops from toasty to freezing, there can be only one conclusion: a seriously pissed-off entity is nearby, and bad things are about to happen.

Repeat this axiom:

"If I see my breath, I'm close to death."

Sample Dialogue: "What's the matter, cat got your ton— . . . Hey, where you going? Hey, I'm talking to you!"

Danger Level: High. Because they're not aware of their ghostly status, there's a good chance they'll inadvertently hurt someone while attempting human activities—driving a cab, for instance.

How to Deal with Them: You probably won't have to. In horror movies, the only humans who can see or hear these ghosts are schizophrenics and sad little boys with single mothers. But on the off chance that you fit one of those descriptions, do not be the one to break the news. You don't want to be within a nuclear mile when that bomb drops.

THE ASSHOLE. Sometimes a person is just an asshole, plain and simple. Ditto for ghosts. Assholes aren't lost between Heaven and Hell. They aren't here to see Junior graduate or settle an old score. They're just hanging around to wreak havoc in the living world. Who knows? Maybe they were wronged somewhere down the line and can't let go. Maybe Daddy missed too many Little League games. It doesn't matter.

Sample Dialogue: "Waahhhh! I'm gonna make your precious earthly lives miserable!"

Danger Level: Extreme. Their sole purpose is to terrorize humans and cause them physical harm—even death.

How to Deal with Them: Move to another state and never return. You can't kill ghosts, and they're next to impossible to trap. The only time you should stand your ground is if you've got a ghoulish ally who's up to the task (only ghosts can hurt other ghosts). But if you are killed, look on the bright side:

Maybe you'll come back as a ghost and get to look at people in the shower.

HOW TO KILL THE LIVING DEAD

Anyone who's killed by a zombie ought to be ashamed of themselves. It's the equivalent of a fighter jet being blown out of the sky with a Nerf dart. Humans are superior to zombies in every imaginable way: We're faster, smarter, stronger, more adaptable, and better looking. And yet, in zombie movies, our so-called heroes hole themselves up in a highly vulnerable location at the first sign of a limper. They sit around scratching their heads and getting hysterical while an army of the dead amasses outside instead of simply planning a counterattack.

```
                    HERO
              (gasping for breath)
     What are we gonna do? There . . .
     there must be two . . . three dozen
     of them in the front yard! At the
     rate they're moving, they'll make
     it to the porch in a few hours!
```

If you're trapped in a movie that pits you against a partially decomposed, laughably uncoordinated enemy, don't retreat: defeat. Just follow these strategies.

1 **STOP BEING SO PATHETIC.** Pull yourself together! You're the human! You possess complex problem-solving skills. You can run faster than a slow shuffle. Stop acting like prey and start acting like a hunter!

Of course you're scared. Your self-confidence has been rattled by fear. So let's puff up that chest and review all the reasons why humans are way, way more awesome than zombies:

> **Speed.** Humans can walk at a good clip. Zombies use tortoises as skateboards. For a while it did seem like fast-moving zombies would be the next big thing in horror movies, but the classic lumbering dead remain by far the most common type.

> **Complex problem-solving abilities.** Humans send robots to Mars. Zombies are baffled by doorknobs.

> **Weaponry.** Humans have a vast supply of guns, knives, chemicals, and explosives at our dexterous fingertips. A zombie's arsenal includes teeth, and . . . wait . . . nope, that's it. Teeth.

> **Strength.** Zombies aren't stronger than humans. On the contrary, their muscles have begun to rot, making them weak and brittle.

2 **ARM YOURSELF.** At the first sign of a zombie outbreak, raid the local gun shops, sporting goods stores, and "we sell everything ever made" megastores, and procure some instruments of undeath.

> **Rifles.** The cornerstone of any anti-zombie campaign. Preferably high-powered semiautomatics.

> **Shotguns.** Excellent for close-quarters fighting. Make heads disappear like magic!

Crossbows. OK, not the most effective weapon against a creature that doesn't care if you poke holes in it. But crossbows are so damn cool . . . why not engage in some bad-assery while you have the chance? Just keep your shotgun handy.

Bombs. Highly effective, whether a brick of C4 or a pipe filled with gunpowder and nails.

Incendiary devices. Zombies are famously terrified of fire, and with good reason—they're much more flammable than we are because their flesh is so dry. And very few manage to stop, drop, and roll once they're been lit.

3 SET A TRAP. Sure, you can roam the countryside for months, taking on zombies one by one. Fighting them with knives and fists. But who has that kind of time? Zombies are cattle. Just drive them to the slaughterhouse. Here's one way of terminating a truckload of dead heads at once.

A Place an explosive device in a confined area, then lure the zombies with fresh brains.

B Wait for the zombies to arrive.

C Detonate the explosives.

D Take cover.

E (Advanced technique) Walk away slowly, not even turning around to look at the explosion because you're that confident.

4 FINISH THE JOB. After the bomb goes off, there'll be bits and pieces of zombie everywhere. But you're not out of danger yet. Here's where those rifles and shotguns come into play. Being careful to keep your ankles away from their mouths, storm the blast area while shooting any remaining zombies full of lead.

5 BURN THE BODIES. Using a push broom or shovel, move the body parts outside, douse them in unleaded gasoline, and roast 'em. Take extreme care to keep their blood and saliva away from your skin, and don't breathe in the resulting smoke—it could still contain traces of the zombie virus.

6 REPEAT AS NEEDED. The great thing about zombies? They'll keep falling for it. Why? Because they're stupid, and we're awesome.

HOW TO KILL A VAMPIRE

They've been horror movie staples since Satan created the Terrorverse and said, "Let there be fright."

Unlike clumsy slashers or tantrum-throwing poltergeists, vampires are graceful. Refined. They don't kill for pleasure or souvenirs, they kill for food—and they're not picky eaters. The young, spry, and infirm are turned into involuntary blood donors in equal numbers. "Anything with a beat is meat," as vampires are fond of saying. Fighting them with your bare hands is suicide. Guns? No effect. Crosses make them laugh. And contrary to popular belief, they're actually quite fond of garlic. But that's not to say that they're invincible. In fact, vampires are among the most vulnerable villains in all of horrordom—as long as you know how to exploit their weaknesses.

1 SET FIRE TO THE LAIR. Every vampire has a safe house, a dark place to crash during those dangerous sunlight hours. These are often crypts, caves, and basements—places that offer plenty of protection from the deadly rays outside. That is, as long as they stay inside.

So how do you get a vampire to leave his lair during the day? Set it on fire. The vampire will wake up with two unsavory options. Option 1: Run outside to escape the fire. Result: Burned to death by sunlight. Option 2: Stay inside to avoid the sunlight. Result: Burned to death by fire.

2 OBTAIN A LICENSE TO BLESS. You want to vanquish a vamp? Graduate from the seminary. Priests have the power to marry couples, preside over services, and, best of all, turn regular water into holy water. And holy water is like battery acid to bloodsuckers. Sure, you could just ask a priest for a few gallons if you didn't feel like going though all the trouble, but a real vampire hunter is locked and loaded with the power of Christ 24/7 and uses that power to preemptively bless as much liquid as possible: swimming pools, bottling plants, rain clouds, even reservoirs.

3 OPEN A 24-HOUR TANNING SALON. Vampires love to look good. Sexy hair. Sculpted bodies. Tailored outfits. But what's the one fashion accessory that's beyond their reach? A healthy tan. Vampires know that the artificial UV rays of a tanning bed won't hurt them. What they don't know is that your tanning beds come with built-in pneumatic stake drivers. Anyone who schedules a tan after midnight has to be a bloodsucker. Sure, you'll kill a few innocents here and there. But if they were tanning in the middle of the night, they were probably very lonely people anyway, and nobody will miss them.

4 MAKE IT THE ANTAGONIST. There are two kinds of vampire movies: ones in which the audience is expected to sympathize with a tortured antihero whose immortality comes at a horrendous cost,

CREATING A SEMI-LIVING WILL

In the Terrorverse, every responsible adult has two wills: one to be carried out in the event of their death, and one to be carried out in the event of their semi-death. It's crucial that you leave your family specific instructions on what to do if you become a zombie, if only to alleviate some of the guilt they might feel about chopping off your head.

Spelling out your wishes in black and white also eliminates the possibility of a painful, protracted legal battle, and ensures that—zombie or not—you'll be allowed to die with some dignity. A semi-living will might be something as simple as this:

Last Semi-Living Will and Testament

I, _____, being of sound, blood-enriched mind and living body, do hereby wish the following three steps to be executed with all due expedience and in the order specified, in the event of my transformation (whether accidental or otherwise) into a zombie:

1. MY HEAD SHALL BE FORCIBLY REMOVED FROM MY BODY.

2. NO LESS THAN FIVE (5) BULLETS SHALL BE FIRED POINT-BLANK FROM A HIGH-POWERED RIFLE INTO MY BRAIN.

3. MY HEAD AND BODY SHALL BE BURNED UNTIL NOTHING BUT ASH REMAINS.

I leave these instructions of my own free will on this day, _____, 20__.

Signed,

_____

and ones in which courageous humans rid themselves of abominable undead predators that shouldn't exist. If you're in the first scenario, your vampiric foe will be undefeatable . . . so switch to the second type ASAP. Spend as much time as possible recounting all the horrible acts and murderous crimes the vampire has committed, loudly and in great detail. Paint your enemy as a monster so heinous that no director would dare allow it to escape retribution for its deeds.

5 **INTERVIEW IT.** Ultimately, a vampire's vanity is its greatest weakness. No bloodsucker can turn down the chance to tell its life story, especially to an author or journalist. You'd think they'd be reclusive—cautious of drawing attention to themselves, lest they stir up any local vampire hunters. But they couldn't care less. They live long, lonely semi-lives. What's the point of it all if they don't have anyone to share it

with? Place an ad like this in the classifieds, and get ready for the phone to start ringing:

How you ambush and kill them when they show up is your choice.

6 **BECOME A VAMPIRE.** It's the nuclear option of anti–vampire warfare. Destroy the enemy, even if it guarantees your own destruction.

Becoming a vampire is easy. Just wander the dark city alleyways (near cemeteries if possible) until one comes along and sinks its fangs into you. As your blood is being drained, request a membership in Club Dead. They'll have you suck blood from them, and before you know it, you'll be craving some red nectar. Once you're transformed, finding other vampires will be easy, since bloodsuckers can smell each other from great distances and you'll be invited to all their parties. And since you're now as fast and as strong as they are, killing them will be easy, too. Of course, the rub of this whole deal is that once you're done killing all the other vampires in your area, you'll have to kill yourself.

HOW TO TELL IF YOU'VE BEEN DEAD SINCE THE BEGINNING OF THE MOVIE

Used to be that a man knew where he stood. Whether he was battling vampires or amorphous blobs, a horror hero could always count on one thing: He was alive. But these days, there's a new dance that's sweeping the Terrorverse: the twist. The shocking revelation at the end of the movie—he's been dead since the 10-minute mark. It's a device that would never be accepted in any other genre.

```
                    SONNY
You mean I . . .

                    (bites fist)
You're tellin' me I never made
it past them tollbooths on the
causeway?
```

To achieve this hoodwink, horror screenwriters give their heroes a condition known as F.R.E.D., Failure to Recognize Earthly Death. If you're trapped in a horror movie, don't take anything for granted, least of all your life.

1 **RETRACE YOUR STEPS.** Were you recently involved in anything that could have sent you to an early grave? A robbery? A car accident? A plane crash? Something you feel lucky to have narrowly survived? Do

you remember what happened immediately afterward? Did you wake up in the hospital surrounded by friends, family, and flowers or is the whole thing a blur? Is there a large chunk of time you simply can't account for? Posttraumatic time loss is a leading indicator of F.R.E.D.

2 ARE YOU BEING HAUNTED? F.R.E.D. victims often experience a phenomenon known as reverse haunting. This occurs when they mistake living people for ghosts—usually a family that's moved into "their" house. Just as ghosts appear solid to certain living people, living people can appear as apparitions to certain ghosts. Ergo, if your condo suddenly becomes infested with ghostly men, women, and children who act like they own the place, they just might.

3 OBSERVE OTHERS. How do others act toward you? Are they rude? Disrespectful of your personal space? Do they fail to hold the door or apologize when they bump into you (and has that been happening a lot)? Do they avoid eye contact unless they're dogs, homeless people, and creepy children? Do your poker buddies always forget to deal you in? Are your kids more standoffish than usual? Does your wife bring strange men home and sleep with them like you're not even there?

The problem may not be your less-than-winning personality, but rather your less-than-detectable pulse.

4 BREAK THE RULES. Being dead has its advantages. For one, you're not governed by rules of common sense and decency. Therefore, one of the surest ways of confirming your death is testing whether or not those rules still apply.

> **Enter restricted areas.** Perhaps a locker room of the opposite sex, a situation room in the Pentagon, or the front of a long line at Starbucks on the first day of pumpkin spice latte season. If no one stops you, you might be dead. Which is probably a better fate than having to drink that latte.

> **Stop flushing.** If no one complains after a few days, there's a solid chance your waste is not of this earth.

> **Root for the Yankees at Fenway.** If you don't die by the seventh-inning stretch, you're already dead.

> **Use the salad fork for your main course.** If no one snickers at your stupidity, all signs point to your morbidity.

> **Wear socks with sandals.** Or black shoes with a brown handbag. If you don't get any disapproving looks from the local fashion police, you're almost certainly dead.

Mess with Texas. No live human being could mess with Texas. If you succeed in messing with Texas, it's a sure bet you're as dead as a June bug in July.

5 **BE SPECIFIC.** Your screenwriter's working overtime to stay one step ahead of today's savvy audience. In order to make it seem as if you're still alive, the writer has to create situations in which people look as if they're responding to you even when they aren't. And to do that, the writer desperately needs you (the hero) to be as vague as possible:

>   HERO
>   Listen, Sam. . . . I know I haven't
>   exactly been the world's best
>   brother, but I just want you to
>   know. I love you.
>
>
>   SAM
>   (looks away, whispers)
>   Why, Liam? Why do bad things
>   happen?

Which means that you should be as specific as possible:

>   HERO
>   What's the square root of nine?
>
>
>   SAM
>   (looks away, whispers)
>   Why, Liam? Why do bad things
>   happen?

⑥ KEEP A TIME JOURNAL. Based on a handful of interviews with F.R.E.D. victims who had recently become aware of their death (but not yet moved on to the next plane) it seems that ghosts experience short "bursts" of existence. Some omnipresent editor reaches in and makes one burst seamlessly flow into the next in such a way that the ghost has no idea that anything out of the ordinary has happened.

Because of this phenomenon, F.R.E.D. victims are notoriously bad at keeping appointments, since their time has little to do with ours. If you're a normally punctual person who suddenly starts missing lunches or wondering where the time went, try keeping a log of your day. Simply write down where you are and what you're doing every half hour for 12 hours, and then review your log in the evening. If you have significantly fewer than 24 entries, there's a chance someone's been cutting out parts of your existence.

⑦ FORCE THE ISSUE. Ultimately, all the journal keeping and specific dialog in the world is no match for a trip to the convenience store. You really want to know if you're dead or not? Stroll into traffic and see if anybody swerves (if you do get hit, go back to step 1 to make sure you weren't killed). Or walk into a vape shop and try to buy an e-cigarette. If the clerk doesn't seem to see or hear you, you're dead. If he does . . . for God's sake, don't actually buy one of those stupid things.

CHAPTER V

MONSTER MASH

ALIENS, BEASTS, AND OTHER WEIRDOS

```
                    NEWT
We'd better get back, 'cause it'll be
dark soon, and they mostly come at
night . . .    mostly.

            —ALIENS (1986)
```

I have to admit . . . I'm rather fond of aliens, possessed beasts, and the like. Unlike some of our clumsier adversaries, there's a certain class to the way they savagely kill. In some ways, it's an honor to be murdered by them. That said, it's an even greater honor to light a victory cigar from their burning corpses.

HOW TO SURVIVE A GLOBAL ALIEN ATTACK

The TV sputters, then quits. Dirty dishes rattle in the sink. An earthquake? Before you even finish the thought, the power cuts out. You open the drapes, letting in the sulfur-yellow glow of streetlights. Then it hits you:

```
                    YOU
        But if the power's out, why are the
        streetlights still . . . ?
```

You notice neighbors gathered in their yards, eyes wide as saucers, pointing at the sky. A sky filled with yellow lights.

And so it begins.

Rumors fly. One hundred ships. One thousand, hovering over every major city in the world. Tanks roll through the streets. World leaders address their anxious flocks. Religious services are standing-room only. Heart attacks and attempted suicides wreak havoc on emergency rooms. And then there's you. Wondering whether to stay, go, or swallow that cyanide capsule you've been saving for just such an emergency.

1 **DON'T BE A SUCKER.** It's a movie rule that dates back to the Truman era: When aliens come to Earth en masse, they do not come in peace. Ever. No matter what olive branch they offer in one purple hand, they're concealing a ray gun in the other. One alien? No problem. You've got yourself the makings of a fine coming-of-age movie. More than one alien? It's a full-scale attack. Guaranteed.

There are only three reasons aliens come in groups:

To eat us. Apparently, humans are quite the scrumptious delicacy. (Though you have to wonder, what do they eat back home?)

To enslave us and steal our resources. Their planet's almost out of crude oil, so they're here to take ours. (Ha, ha! Joke's on them!)

To destroy us for no reason. That is, other than the fact that they're total dicks. Dicks who (after eons of evolution, philosophical discussion, and scientific advancement) have decided that the meaning of it all is to kill.

Never trust an alien. Not even if they give you the cure for cancer wrapped in the end of world hunger. Don't you realize they're just making sure we're plump and tumor-free?

POOR CAREER CHOICES FOR HORROR MOVIE CHARACTERS

Surviving a horror movie is hard enough without choosing one of these 99.9 percent fatal professions:

A) **GRAVEDIGGER.** A job that requires you to dig graves. In a cemetery. Alone.

B) **POLAR SCIENTIST.** "Hey, I know—I'll go to the most isolated part of the world. A place where night lasts for six months! What a great idea!"

C) **SECURITY GUARD.** If something goes bump in the night, you're the guy who has to check it out.

D) **CAMP DIRECTOR.** You're an authority figure who bosses teenagers around in the middle of the woods. It's a shock you lived long enough to read this senten— . . .

E) **JANITOR.** Strange. You could've sworn you locked the door to the pool. Why are the lights off? And why does that laughter sound like it's coming from the water?

F) **HOOKER.** Prostitution is so fatal in movies that hookers rarely even get the courtesy of an on-screen death. The first time we see them is when our grizzled hero cop is scraping them out of several Dumpsters.

2 STAY AWAY FROM THE SHIPS. Let those flute-playing hippies
be the first to feel the aliens' wrath. "Oh, look! They're flashing some
lights! Aren't they pretty? I wonder what's gonna happen next?" Allow
me to ruin the surprise: You're going to be blasted with a Xoraxian
Krellbor that turns your bones into lava.

3 LOOT. You might think that looting is wrong, but when the ships
begin firing, you can drive over to the local megastore and wait
patiently for one of the cashiers to show up for work. And when you
finally grow a brain and realize that civilization is closed until further
notice, throw a shopping cart through the window and start grabbing
supplies:

Food. Dry, canned, and powdered only. As much as you can carry.

A pistol. And plenty of ammo. Not for fighting aliens—for protecting yourself from humans who decide they want some of
your supplies.

Camping equipment. Tents, sleeping bags, flashlights, waterproof
matches, hand-cranked radios, binoculars, knives, propane tanks,
blankets, batteries, and rope.

First aid supplies. Bandages, hydrogen peroxide, and pain reliev-
ers are priorities.

Large-capacity squirt guns. Refer to the explanation in step 5
on page 131.

4 RETREAT TO A REMOTE LOCATION. Even the biggest alien inva-
sions are limited to urban areas, at least during the first phase. If
they're here to eat us, that's where the most people are. If they're here to

enslave us, that's where our heads of state are. And if they're just dicks, that's where they can do the most damage in the shortest amount of time.

You have no business being anywhere near a metropolitan area. If you're in a tiny, long-forgotten town that you've been dreaming of leaving your whole life, stay there. If you're a city dweller who drives into the surrounding countryside and makes snarky remarks like "Can you believe people live out here?", go live out there.

GOOD REMOTE LOCATIONS:

Woods (spring and summer). Leafy treetops provide excellent cover, and abundant wildlife provides food when the canned stuff runs out.

Caves (fall and winter). There's a reason we lived in them for thousands of years. They're easy to heat, they protect you from the elements, and they keep you well hidden. The deeper the cave, the better.

BAD REMOTE LOCATIONS:

Cornfields. These are probably being used as terrain markers or staging areas for the invaders. Besides, a cornfield is one of the last places you want to be in a horror movie (see "What to Do If Your Corn Has Children in It," page 148).

Prairies. Wide open spaces have no hiding places.

5 STAY CLOSE TO WATER. If you have a boat, now would be the time to get something more practical than a superiority complex out of it. Aliens tend to ignore the 70 percent of our planet covered in water. Drive a few miles offshore and wait this whole mess out if you have the option. If you have access to a submarine, even better.

If the closest you can get to water is the puddle that forms on the roof of your tent, fear not. Remember those large-capacity squirt guns you looted? Fill them up and keep them close at all times. If you run into a spaceman, you stand a better chance of killing it with a good soaking than a hail of bullets. Alien invasion movies are basically metaphors for man's overreliance on technology, so it's almost always something primitive that brings the aliens to their knees. Earthly bacteria, bee stings, or water. Or maybe a loud noise.

                    ZORAC
          Prepare the fleet! The blue planet
          shall be ours!

                    CROM
          But the blue planet is covered in
          korlock!

                    ZORAC
          So?

                    CROM
          So, doesn't korlock turn our
          syndaks into meklar?

                    ZORAC
                  (thinks)
          Good point.
                    (to others)
          OK, everybody hear that? Stay away
          from the korlock parts.

```
                    CROM
    But you can't just . . .


                    ZORAC
    ENGAGE!
```

WHAT TO DO
IF IT FOLLOWS YOU

For all that the Terrorverse loves to repurpose monsters—if it ain't broke, why not sequel it?—there's always a chance you'll find yourself beset by some new, previously uncategorized threat. It might be a space alien; it might be a one-off supernatural weirdo; it might be some unexplained, unseen thing that you can't look at (thus sparing the film's special effects budget). The good news is that this new "It" will be unfamiliar to the audience, too, so the movie will need to spend time laying out the rules of the game. During this stage of the story, you'll probably be followed around and occasionally startled by a disguised, mostly obscured, or perhaps invisible menace. Use this time to implement your defense.

1 **SEEK SAFETY IN NUMBERS.** In movies of this type, characters typically learn how It operates as It munches its way through the cast like they're a bag of Doritos. If you're alone, you'll become one more corpse for the others to find and learn from ("Hmmm, Bob's pants were left untouched . . . the creature must be vulnerable to polyester!"). In a group, you have a chance at being the last one left standing.

Especially if you surround yourself with these types:

A few scientists or academics. The movie doesn't have all day; someone has to put the pieces together and figure out what makes It tick, and the eggheads can really move the conversation along. Once the creature's nature is revealed, though, they're dead meat.

An especially aggravating asshole. In the Terrorverse, people who are abrasive, argumentative, or unlikeable might as well have targets on their backs. The audience loves seeing them get their comeuppance in the bloodiest of ways . . . and better them than you.

A child. Kids are often imperiled in the Terrorverse, but an on-screen death is rare, so stay close. Don't fall into the trap of sacrificing yourself to save the kid, though; the child will survive no matter what, so there's no reason for such heroism. Bonus points if the little tyke has a distinctive feature like a disability or psychic power, because this will likely be the key to beating the monster.

A cop or soldier. Or even a physical trainer. Someone who's strong, confident, and an experienced fighter will help the group get through the early scenes of the movie . . . and after the first act, that tough guy or gal will be the first to go, in order to make everyone more vulnerable.

Optimists or pessimists. The Terrorverse abhors certainty. Characters who constantly declare that everything will be all right in the end will be proven wrong and quickly ended. Those who spend most of their time huddled in a corner convinced that this is game over, man, will last longer. But eventually the movie will kill them off to put an end to their whining.

2 **PAY ATTENTION.** So that evil-looking book that you didn't even buy keeps reappearing in different parts of your house? Or people in your neighborhood are inexplicably turning up dead with their legs bent backward? Such warning signs would be cause for alarm in the real world, but in the Terrorverse people inexplicably ignore them. Don't be like that! These are clues to the nature of the threat that's coming.

3 **SEEK A RESTRAINING ORDER.** Even if it's just a mysterious swirl of leaves, there's no reason to put up with some otherworldly creep following you everywhere you go. Everyone, even a relentless predator from another dimension, fears lawyers.

KNOW YOUR HARBINGERS
OF IMPENDING DOOM:
THE HEAD TILT

In everyday circumstances, the human head tends to be upright. It might tilt forward if someone's drowsy, or backward if somebody wants to check out some neat skywriting. A head might rotate left or right, or nod, or shake back and forth in time with music. This is all normal. A thing that ordinary, sane, harmless people do *not* do with their head is tilt it slowly sideways, like a confused dog, moving their ear close to their shoulder, and then holding that position for several seconds or more. This behavior is the province of crazy people, the possessed, and disguised abominations that don't really understand how humans behave. The degree of the head tilt (either left or right) indicates how much danger you're in:

0–10 DEGREES: Minimal danger; person is puzzled or has an inner ear infection

11–30 DEGREES : Mild danger; person has sociopathic tendencies

31–45 DEGREES: Significant danger; a serial killer is sizing you up

45–60 DEGREES: Extreme danger; this is a mutant or an animated corpse

61+ DEGREES: The human neck doesn't allow this, why are you still standing there?

NOTE: If head tilt is accompanied by the slow crescendo of stringed instruments, the danger increases by one level.

4 PREY ON ITS INSECURITIES. You're dealing with a new kind of monster, one desperate to achieve Dracula-level (or at least Mummy-level) fame. Try to shake It's confidence by pointing out the inconsistencies in the creature's backstory. ("If you're so sensitive to noise, why'd you come to such a noisy planet?") Make up some insulting quotes from famous directors. ("Did you hear that Quentin Tarantino called you boring and fat?") Or just misidentify It. ("So, you're basically a ghost who can't talk, right?")

5 LEAD IT SOMEPLACE BORING. After a few visits to the Museum of Paperclips, Jo-Ann Fabrics, or your aunt's house, It will probably go in search of someone else to follow.

10 WILDLIFE CREATURES
THAT ARE ALWAYS EVIL

1. **MONKEYS.** Opportunistic bastards. A monkey would sell its own mother for a stale banana peel—which is why they're always recruited as spies for the enemy.

2. **ROTTWEILERS.** Dogs are universally good, with one exception. It seems that Rottweilers put their paw print on a contract with Satan, since they're always portrayed as rabid psychopaths or guardians of the Antichrist.

3. **SHARKS.** In the real world, they're scary looking but mostly harmless and threatened by extinction. In horror movies, sharks crave human flesh, can carry a grudge, solve problems, eat boats, and track people halfway across the globe.

4. **RAVENS.** As birds go, ravens are actually quite pleasant. Unfortunately, they're also classic harbingers of impending doom.

5. **CATS.** Whereas monkeys are evil because it pays well, cats are just plain evil. They don't need an incentive to sell you out or steal your baby's breath; they do it for the sheer pleasure of being rotten.

6. **RATS.** Where there's one rat, there's 14,000. And where there's 14,000 rats, there's some sociopath using them to murder people.

7. **BATS.** It's not a bat, it's a vampire.

8. **OWLS.** Owls have been waging a PR campaign to change their perennial image as evil creatures. They've bought their way into a few family films, playing the faithful friend or endangered species, but don't be fooled—they're coldhearted killers.

9. **SLOTHS.** There's actually nothing to suggest sloths are evil. But isn't it suspicious how popular they've become in recent years? Plus they're the only animal named after a deadly sin. Probably best to avoid them.

10. **WOLVES.** It's not a wolf, it's a werewolf.

HOW TO SURVIVE A SPACE-BASED HORROR MOVIE

Isolation. The secret sauce that makes horror movies so deliciously unnerving. It can be physical (a remote cabin, a snowbound hotel), metaphysical (insanity, the afterlife), or both. But nothing compares to the isolation of space.

Rescue could be light years away. Running outside isn't an option. And what you're up against never has fewer than two mouths. Worse yet, space-based horror movies are among the most expensive to produce—meaning their writers and directors are a cut above direct-to-video. And the more talented your filmmaking adversaries, the more likely that the final frontier will become your final resting place.

1 NEVER ANSWER A DISTRESS SIGNAL. Why would you ever go to a place where people are in trouble? In horror movies, "Help!" doesn't translate to "Our hyperdrive is on the fritz again." It means, "No one else lived long enough to send this message." By the time you arrive, not only will everyone be dead, but whatever killed them will be hungry. This is precisely why caller ID was invented.

>   COMMUNICATIONS OFFICER
>   Captain! A distress signal from
>   the orphan transport vessel Charity
>   7! They say something strange is
>   happening to the orphans!
>
>
>   CAPTAIN
>   Yeah, um . . . let that one go to
>   voicemail.

2 NEVER INVESTIGATE A FAILURE TO RESPOND. The only thing more ominous than a distress signal is no signal.

† If a distant colony stops transmitting, the colonists are dead. Make no attempts to recover bodies or equipment. Proceed to step 7.

† If a ship doesn't respond to hails, either the crew is dead or they've been driven insane by some faceless evil from another dimension, and will eat the soul of anyone who boards. Proceed to step 7.

† If a fellow crew member doesn't answer the intercom, a liquid formerly known as your shipmate is being vomited onto the engine room floor after disagreeing with an alien's stomach. If he or she was in a section that can be remotely jettisoned, you might want to go ahead and do that. Otherwise, pull the self-destruct handle and book it to the nearest escape pod.

3 NEVER EXPLORE AN UNEXPLORED PLANET. This isn't science fiction. Strange new worlds aren't inhabited by talking monkeys or technologically gifted, sexy utopian women. They're cold, dark rocks harboring terrible secrets—secrets that gobble up your crew one by one. If you happen upon a world that isn't listed in the Pocket Planetary Atlas, keep on truckin'.

4 NEVER GO THROUGH A WORMHOLE. Some things are best left unknown.

Writers have been trying to hammer that one home since Pandora's curiosity first brought evil into the world—all because she simply had to know what was in that box. And yet horror movie characters continue to ask, sometimes in the most demanding terms:

"What's in the box?"

Wormholes are essentially shortcuts through hundreds, millions, or even billions of light years of space. Like Pandora, you might stare into those luminescent ripples of dark matter and wonder what's on the other side. Think of the stories you'd be able to tell. You'd be the Magellan of the modern era. All you have to do is move ever so slightly forward and break the surface. And so you do. And just as light and time begin to take on the turquoise hue of impossible speed, you have a moment of nauseating clarity: "Wait a second . . . I'm in a horror moviiiiieeeeeeeeee." It's too late.

5 TURN ON THE LIGHTS. According to space-based horror movies, sometime in the not-too-distant future, ship design is going to take a quantum leap in stupidity. Fed up with building brightly lit, space-saving vessels, designers are going to add deck after useless deck to their increasingly mammoth tankers of the galaxy. These fusion guzzlers will have random steam-belching pipes, rotating beacon lights, and an endless supply of hiding places—but a very limited supply of lightbulbs.

The director and cinematographer are at it again—sacrificing realism for mood and increasing the scare factor by decreasing the illumination. But you can fight back without even leaving the bridge.

```
                    YOU
        Computer, set all onboard lights to
        100 percent.


                  COMPUTER (V.O.)
        Are you sure? That seems awfully
        inefficient.


                    YOU
        And the fact that this ship has 26
        decks for five crew members? That
        isn't inefficient?
```

```
              COMPUTER (V.O.)
        Good point. Raising lights.
```

6 KNOW WHEN TO ABANDON SHIP. The filmmakers want you to see this thing through to the bitter end. Save the nobility for real life. There's no shame in heading for that escape pod at the first hint of danger, such as:

> **Anything pops out of anybody's chest.** Whether it's an alien or the Tootsie Roll owl, get the hell out of there.

> **You're on a rescue mission.** This has already been covered. There's no such thing as a rescue in space. You're merely the second wave of victims.

> **Your dead wife is walking around the ship.** You're going crazy, and the ship wants you to go even crazier. Leave immediately.

> **You can't stop building things with mashed potatoes.** Actually, you should stick around for this one, it's pretty cool.

7 NUKE ANYTHING THAT EVEN REMOTELY CREEPS YOU OUT. It's the only way to be sure.

THE PRE-HYPERSLEEP CHECKLIST

Do you lock the doors before you go to bed? Of course you do. We're vulnerable while we sleep, so we take precautions. But what if you're planning on sleeping longer than eight hours? What if you're going to snooze for two or more years? Your precautions need to be more thorough than locking the door. If you're about to take a hypernap, don't rest until every one of these boxes is checked:

☐ Scanners detect no unidentified life-forms or movement aboard.

☐ Crew and passenger ultrasounds are negative for alien embryos.

☐ Ship's computer has no secret instructions to terminate life support.

☐ Women are dressed in sexy cotton undergarments.

☐ Plotted course doesn't pass through any asteroid belts, stars, or black holes.

☐ Coffeemaker is set to start brewing 10 minutes before alarm clock.

THE SATANIC "VERSUS"

CURSES, WITCHES, AND THE DEVIL HIMSELF

REGAN
What an excellent day for an exorcism.

—THE EXORCIST (1973)

(Sung to Simon and Garfunkel's "The Sound of Silence"): Hello Satan, my old friend. I've come to fight with you again. Because you're worse than any poltergeist. You turn our kids into the Antichrist. And the demon, that you planted in that girl—made her hurl. Now hear my sound . . . of violence.

WHAT TO DO IF YOUR CORN HAS CHILDREN IN IT

Not only is farming one of the deadliest horror occupations (remoteness, animals, sharp things everywhere), but in the hands of most screenwriters, cornstalks are antennas for receiving evil. Why? Because they're a clear metaphor for isolation, easy to get lost in, cheap to film in, and—best of all—very, very hard to see in. Because cornfields are such ripe horror territory, they're often infested with demons, sign-making aliens, winged carnivores, and worst of all . . . fanatical children.

A religious child infestation is every corn farmer's worst nightmare. The onset is sudden, and the results can be disastrous for the crops. If left untreated, the little buggers will make themselves at home, using inventory to make crucifixes, trampling paths everywhere, and chanting Bible passages day and night. If your infestation has already progressed to conducting human sacrifices and summoning false gods, burn the whole mess and collect government subsidies until next season. But if you've caught it early enough, here are some safe, somewhat humane ways of driving them out, each step increasing in severity.

1 **FIRE UP THE CROP DUSTER.** Farmers use aircraft to spray their fields with bug-killing chemicals. You can employ the same method to counter the effects of corn-dwelling kids. But instead of spraying pesticides, you'll need to blanket the infected area with something that neutralizes naughty children. Some suggestions:

> **Crushed Ritalin.** Nothing soothes the savage preteen like a bloodstream full of methylphenidate. Get your hands on several cases of Ritalin, mill it into a fine powder, and dust away.

Before you know it, the little buggers will be off to find the nearest Sylvan Learning Center. About 40 pills per child should do the trick.

A skimpy tank top. Due to their religious fanaticism, corn-dwelling children dress like eighteenth-century puritans—a weakness easily exploited with a single piece of twenty-first-century clothing. One of the female pests will happen upon the tank top and try it on, instantly making her the hottest girl in the cornfield. The other females will divide into two groups: those who befriend the girl to bask in her popularity, and those who denounce her as a "total whore." The males, meanwhile, will practically tear one another apart trying to be with her. Result? What had been a harmonious, God-fearing community is now a John Hughes movie, and the colony destroys itself from within.

Pot brownies. It doesn't matter what kind of demon they have protecting them, nothing has more power over a child than the smell of fresh-baked brownies—especially when you've been gnawing on nothing but raw corn for months. Drop a few pot-laced batches (you're on your own when it comes to scoring the ingredients) over the focal point of the infestation and wait for the hungry vermin to gobble them up. When you hear "Redemption Song" or "Comfortably Numb" in the distance, that's your cue to drive into the field, round them up (they won't resist), and dump them at the nearest 24-hour diner, where they'll share a plate of gravy fries and talk about death till the sun comes up.

2 **BUILD A BASEBALL FIELD.** If crop dusting comes up short, don't despair. In the late 1980s, a loophole was created in the "all movie cornfields are evil" law, and you can reap the benefits with only a small investment of time and money.

First, clear a few acres of your corn, preferably near your farmhouse.

Next, build a baseball field. You'll need some dirt, chalk, fencing (for the backstop), a few poles, some lights, and, of course, regulation bases. The whole shebang shouldn't run more than a few hundred thousand dollars, assuming you do the labor yourself.

Once the field is complete, it shouldn't be more than a few days before deceased Hall-of-Famers show up for practice. At this point, your cornfield has been transformed from evil to merely enchanted, and the children will be forced to leave.

A word of warning: If you leave the baseball field up too long, you'll be swarmed with motorists who felt compelled to drive all the way to your farm to see it. You also run the risk of your dead father showing up.

3 CONDUCT AUDITORY WARFARE.

In 1989, the United States invaded Panama and cornered dictator Manuel Noriega, who'd taken refuge in the Vatican Embassy. Since they couldn't enter the embassy without permission, the Army turned to an alternative weapon—rock and roll. Using a huge speaker, they blasted the building with ear-piercing music. Eventually, Noriega surrendered. (In 1993, the U.S. government tried a similar thing during the Waco standoff, with less desirable results.)

Aim a group of giant concert speakers at the infested area and blast the most child-repellent noise you can think of. The vermin will either be driven out or driven insane, which is a win-win situation as far as you're concerned. A few playlist possibilities:

> **The O'Reilly Factor for Kids audiobook.** Imagine the horror of getting advice on being a teenager from the 50-something who wrote this: "The adult doesn't have to be in the room snappin' to OutKast, but one of these specimens must be somewhere on the premises."

Jimmy Buffett's "Margaritaville." Scientists have proven that listening to this song causes acute hemorrhaging of the eardrums in anyone under 47.

Old people complaining. Nothing is more aggravating to kids than listening to their parents and grandparents tell the same sob stories of how hard life was when they were young. Simply recruit an old person, give them a microphone, and get them to babble about any of the following: their polio-stricken little brother or sister, the war, or their alcoholic father who lost his job at the plant and beat them with a belt.

FOUR WAYS TO HANDLE A WITCH

There was a time when witches were so feared that an accusation of witchcraft could ruin someone's reputation . . . and by "reputation" we mean "life," and by "ruin" we mean "end via prolonged torture, imprisonment, and gruesome public execution." Later they were relegated to children's storybooks, Disney movies, and Halloween decorations. Then they became fodder for TV sitcoms and Broadway musicals. These days, the Terrorverse is bringing back the primal, scary, cook-you-in-a-cauldron-and-ask-questions-never type of witch. Here's what you need to do to stay safe.

1 BE NICE TO OLD PEOPLE. Any woman, or sometimes man, over the age of 45 is a potential witch, because why else would they be there? Horror movies, like all contemporary entertainment media, prefer to populate the screen with young, attractive people. So treat all olds with caution, and if you encounter one dressed as a carnival fortune teller, witchdom is a 98 percent certainty. Insulting this person—mocking her supermarket-purchased reading glasses, denying her a bank loan, running her over with your car—will result in a curse that lands you in hell or someplace like it (graduate school?).

2 MAKE FRIENDS WITH THE AMISH. Or if not the Amish, some other traditionalist community that still remembers the Old Ways. Every type of magic has a counterspell, but you probably have no idea how to paint a hex sign or what kind of animal entrails to hang over your front door to block a curse. While it's true that insular religious groups are distrustful of outsiders, they'll help you anyway just for the satisfaction of seeing your modern know-how being proven useless.

3 CUT A DEAL. One thing about witches: they're busy people. Their job involves lots of tedious prep time—mixing potions, digging up mandrake roots, hunting around for black hares and unbaptized babies, not to mention labeling all those mason jars. So there's always a chance the witch will give you a break in exchange for taking something off her to-do list. True, you may end up trudging through a marsh at midnight in search of a three-eyed toad. But that's better than being turned *into* a toad.

4 PULL A S-WITCH-EROO. The witch is a character type that crosses genres, so in a pinch you might be able to jump the movie onto another track. Try romancing the witch; for the cost of a bottle of wine and dinner at a fancy restaurant, you could find yourself in a delightful romantic comedy about a witch and a mortal trying to make it work. Bring in a plucky kid with a heart of gold, and possibly a pet dog, and now you have a children's movie in which the evil witch is destined to

fail. Or use your phone to film yourself wandering around talking to the camera about how lost and scared you are. Now you're in a fake documentary in which the witch never appears on-screen and may not even be real.

HOW TO PERFORM AN EXORCISM

As powerful as they are, demons lack one thing we puny humans take for granted: a body. But every so often, Satan paroles an inmate and sends it topside with explicit instructions: Hijack a vulnerable human body. What does Beelzebub want with a measly meat puppet, anyway? Simple. The scales of good and evil are precariously balanced. Tip them ever so slightly in one direction (a handful of demons taking human form will do it), and before long, God's on the ropes.

Spend enough time in the Terrorverse, and you'll encounter a human who's the subject of a hostile takeover. When you do, it's important to act quickly and decisively, because the fate of the world (and perhaps all of existence) is in your hands. So keep your cool, and know your rites.

1 **CONFIRM THE NEED FOR AN EXORCISM.** You don't want to go through all the trouble of carrying out an ancient ritual only to discover your supposed victim merely neglected to take their meds. The Catholic Church created strict guidelines for the rite of exorcism back in 1614—guidelines that have remained largely unchanged in 400 years. However, one notable amendment came in 1952, when priests were warned not to confuse mental illness with demonic possession

(as opposed to the old days, when the two were inseparable). Look for the following signs to determine that an exorcism is more urgent than a shrink.

Telepathy. A demon will be able to mine your thoughts for fears, regrets, and embarrassing details as well as project nightmarish visions into your head. It may also be able to predict the future.

Telekinesis. Demons have the ability to mentally manipulate objects—making doors slam, shaking beds, hurling knives across the room, etc.

Language. When possessed, victims are fluent in languages they've never studied (usually Latin). They may also have the ability to speak backward or in multiple voices.

Appearance. Eyes that have changed color or gone completely white and skin that is pale and covered in lacerations are sure signs of demonic possession.

2 GATHER THE REQUIRED TOOLS.
You're going to need help, and lots of it. According to the rites of exorcism, only an ordained Catholic priest can perform the ritual. So the first "tool" you'll need is a man of the cloth. The rites call for an older, morally pristine specimen. But forget the older part—performing an exorcism is like going 12 rounds with Ivan Drago. The elderly need not apply. Your priest should be in killer shape—well rested, with zero emotional baggage. No recently deceased parents, no scandals, and no deep insecurities. If he's hiding anything, the demon will sniff it out in a heartbeat, and your padre will be at risk of becoming possessed himself.

The next "tool" is a physician. Both you and the victim are likely to get some cuts and bruises during the exorcism. It's best to have an able-bodied M.D. on hand, just in case. The doctor should be the same sex as the victim (to avoid any scandalous touching that might empower the demon).

And then there's you. You'll be on hand to provide whatever physical and moral support you can, beginning with gathering the following items:

Bible. These can be found in most hotel rooms.

Crucifix. Not too big or too sharp.

Holy water. By the bucket.

Surgical masks, gloves, and rubber boots. Blood and vomit will be flying.

Rope. For tying the victim to the bed, and for tying the bed to the floor.

Warm clothes. The temperature is bound to drop as the demon does everything it can to make you uncomfortable.

Fresh coffee. It's going to be a long night. Keep the pot full.

③ PREPARE THE ROOM. First and foremost, the room should be on the ground floor. Too many priests have been lost as the result of accidental or intentional leaps from high windows. If the victim's bedroom, often the easiest place to stage an exorcism, is on an upper floor, move the victim to a bedroom on the ground floor. Place a plastic drop cloth on the floor and set all the collected tools within easy reach. Finally, remove all occult objects. Some of these may seem innocent, but to the trained exorcist, they're express lanes to downtown Hell:

Stuffed animals. Children practically worship their precious bears and ponies. Such idolatry is expressly forbidden by the Ten Commandments.

Dungeons & Dragons. A game created by the Dark Lord to lure young nerds into his service.

Harry Potter books. Never mind that the letters in "Harry Potter" can be rearranged to spell "Thy Terror, Pa!" ("Pa" is an obvious reference to God.) These books encourage young readers to imagine a world filled with ghosts, witches, and naughty children. And imagination is the devil's playground.

Non-Christian albums. These are music to Satan's ears.

Computers. The Internet is a haven for smut peddlers and secularist bloggers.

4 START WITH A PRAYER. Any prayer will do. Make sure to ask for God's divine assistance with the difficult task ahead, and profess your personal unworthiness as a sinner a few times. Throw in a little Latin for seasoning.

5 TAKE ROLL CALL. Place one hand on the Bible and the other on the victim's forehead. Command that any demons present reveal themselves. The demon will begin to resist. Ignore it and continue to step 6.

6 READ SCRIPTURE. The following passages are recommended in the Catholic Church's official rites:

John 1:14. "The Word became flesh and made his dwelling among us. We have seen his glory, the glory of the One and Only, who came from the Father, full of grace and truth."

Mark 16:17. "And these signs will accompany those who believe: In my name they will drive out demons; they will speak in new tongues."

Luke 10:17-18. "The seventy-two returned with joy and said, 'Lord, even the demons submit to us in your name.' He replied, 'I saw Satan fall like lightning from heaven.'"

Back page of church bulletin. "Please register if you're bringing something to next week's bake sale. Last year we had too much banana bread."

7 COMMAND THE DEMON TO LEAVE THE VICTIM'S BODY.

This is where the priest's voice should reach full fire-and-brimstone pitch. Make repeated references to the power of Christ. Repeat this phrase over and over again: "Depart then, impious one! Depart, accursed one! Depart with all your deceits, for God has willed that man should be his temple!"

8 BE READY FOR DEMONIC COUNTERATTACKS

Your demonic foe won't go quietly into that eternal night. It'll do everything in its considerable power to confuse, tire, anger, and manipulate you. If given the chance, it'll kill you, too. Everyone on the exorcism team needs to stay focused if there's to be any hope of success. And to do that, they need to know what's coming:

Personal insights. Nothing that comes out of the victim's mouth (including vomit) should be given a second thought, no matter how personal or painful it is to hear.

Visions. Don't take anything you see at face value, no matter how real it seems. This includes the appearance of dead friends, dreamlike flashes of hideous faces, and images of your own death.

Vulgarity. Catholic priests are celibate, and there's nothing demons love more than pushing those dusty buttons to make them sweat. Be ready for pornographic dialogue.

Displays of power. Levitation, window rattling, temperature fluctuations, electrical disturbances, appearance changes, furniture moves, and head spinning, to name a few.

9 MAKE SURE THE DEMON'S REALLY GONE.

Sometimes, those tricky little hellions will pretend to flee in the name of Christ when in fact they're just laying low until you leave. So before you go ahead and proclaim victory over the armies of the damned, it would behoove you to conduct a few experiments to confirm the total absence of the demon:

Have the victim take communion. Minions of Satan don't react well to the Eucharist.

Take the victim to a zoo. If the animals become uneasy, you've still got a problem.

Give the victim a bath. Don't tell them that they're bathing in holy water! If they do fine, the demon's fled.

WHAT TO DO IF YOU HAVE ONLY SEVEN DAYS TO LIVE

There's an old axiom, "Tomorrow is promised to no one." Well, that goes quadruple in the Terrorverse, especially when you do something to raise the ire of the Reaper. Maybe you watched a cursed videotape on a dare. Maybe you escaped some gruesome fate you weren't meant to escape. Or maybe Death just has a grudge against you. When your flight to the afterlife switches from "delayed" to "now boarding," adopt one of two philosophies:

"A dying man needs to die, as a sleepy man needs to sleep, and there comes a time when it is wrong, as well as useless, to resist."
—Stewart Alsop

Or

"'Tis very certain the desire of life prolongs it."
—Lord Byron

If you decide that it's useless to resist, don't waste another precious minute reading mediocre metafiction. Get out there and live the next seven days like you've never lived before. But if you agree that the desire for life prolongs it, spend each day as follows:

DAY 1 HAVE A GOOD CRY. You deserve it. Finding out you have only a week to live is a good excuse to throw a pity party. Take a day to curl up with a box of tissues, a container of rocky road, and the dulcet tones of Oprah. Feel sorry for yourself. Feel scared. Feel free to get stinking drunk.

Better? Good. Now get over it, you pathetic mess.

DAY 2 PARTNER UP AND START SLEUTHING. If you're going to beat death, you're going to have to face it head-on, and you're in no condition to do it alone. You'll need a partner, preferably an uncursed person of the opposite sex, who will bring some much-needed perspective to the situation. Plus, you'll get to sleep with her later in the movie. Everybody wins (including the audience).

Together you should set off investigating the source of the curse. But before you hit the road, get on the Internet. Horror movie characters usually find valuable information online—especially if they're in a sequel.

```
                    YOU
My God . . . look at this.
          (clicks mouse)
There are hundreds of Web sites and
message boards about people who've
died after saying those magic
words. Boy, if only I'd learned to
use a computer before today, huh?
```

Armed with whatever information you can find, start pounding the pavement looking for additional clues. Return to the tomb you raided or track down the relatives of other victims. The hope is that you'll follow the breadcrumbs all the way to the source of the curse's power and find some way to appease it, thus lifting your death sentence.

DAY 3 STALL THE FILMMAKERS. If your investigation hasn't met with any success by Day 3, it's time to think about slowing this process down. Trip up the filmmakers using these passage of time countermeasures:

Dress in period costume. Viewers will wonder if they're watching a flashback.

Stay away from clocks and calendars. Instruments such as these make it all too easy for the director to illustrate the passage of time.

Avoid montage-related activities. The last thing you need right now is a montage to burn through a few days in matter of minutes. (For a guide to montage activities, see page 67.)

Don't waste time sleeping. You probably skimmed "How to Stay Awake for a Week" (page 66), thinking, "I'll never need this." Well, you need it now. Every moment spent snoozing is a moment on the cutting room floor.

Keep talking. Especially when you're on the move. Filmmakers tend to condense travel into a few shots. But if you continue spewing dialogue while you're on the move—especially dialogue relevant to the story—they'll be forced to keep it in the final cut.

DAY 4

SET YOUR AFFAIRS IN ORDER. If you haven't solved this thing by day four, it's time to consider the possibility that you're not being asked back for the sequel. I'm not telling you to admit defeat—not by a long shot. But I am telling you to be smart. To get a few things out of the way while there's still time:

† Create or update your will.

† Write your memoirs.

† Tell the people you love that you love them.

† Tell the people you hate that you hate them.

† Make any necessary religious pilgrimages or preparations.

† Go skydiving.

† Spend an obscene amount of money on yourself.

† Give an obscene amount of money to a hobo.

† Kill the hobo with your bare hands just to see what it feels like.

DAY 5

TRY TO CUT A DEAL. Things aren't looking good. Fighting death head-on is getting you nowhere.

Maybe you're going about this whole thing the wrong way. Maybe you should be negotiating with death. Maybe there's something you can do for death in exchange for getting the curse lifted. Carry out some kind of errand? Pass the curse to others? Kill a hobo? Wait . . . you already did that. Point is, this is a horror movie. Death is everywhere. If you want to talk to it, all you have to do is close your eyes and open your mouth.

Wait till nightfall, find a nice, spooky place with no one else around, and invite death to the bargaining table. Just close your eyes and speak into the darkness:

```
                    YOU
    Um, Mr. Reaper? Grim? You there?
    It's me. The one who you're coming
    for in 48 hours. Listen, um . . .
    I was wondering . . . is there some
    kind of arrangement we might be
    able to work out? Quid pro quo? I
    scratch your robe, you scratch mine?
            (nervous laughter)
    Death? Hello?
```

Since you're in a movie, death will give a clear signal if the answer is "yes." A candle will blow out, a wolf will howl, or (if the filmmakers are feeling uninspired) the word "yes" will write itself in a foggy mirror. If that's the case, great. Let the negotiations begin. If not . . .

DAY 6 **HAVE ANOTHER GOOD CRY.** Other than praying for a favorable last-minute plot twist, there's not much that can be done. You might as well enjoy what little time you have left. Are there any items on your Day 4 list that you didn't get to?

DAY 7

FIND A DELOREAN. You're probably going to die today, my friend. Don't feel bad. You tried. But in the end, "Tomorrow is promised to no one," right?

It's time for one last cross-genre Hail Mary pass: time travel. Find a local scientist, physics professor, or inventor, and beg for help in throwing together a time machine (assuming there isn't a DeLorean in the garage already). If you manage to build it fast enough (before the screenwriter gets wind of what's happening), it just might work.

Using the machine, go at least one week forward or backward. If you go backward, you can avoid doing whatever it was that got you in this mess in the first place. If you go forward, then technically you've lived longer than the one-week limit on your life, and beaten the curse.

HOW TO DEFEAT SATAN

In the unlikely event that you've read this book from beginning to end, you've learned how to deal with some pretty unsavory characters. But nothing you've faced so far can come close to preparing you for the most dangerous character the Terrorverse has to offer:

The devil himself.

This isn't some second-rate demon moonlighting as a little girl. It's not a clumsy wisecracking slasher or a killer doll. This is Satan, people. Lucifer. Mephistopheles, if you will.

Take every bad thing that's ever happened since the dawn of time—every injustice, every murder, every war, every tragedy, and every broken heart. Multiply the sum total of all that pain to the 48 billionth power, and you have roughly the amount of evil Satan sprinkles over his morning cereal.

The point is: Satan is very, very evil.

And not just evil—all-powerful. Pound for pound, el Diablo is every bit as omnipotent as God (in the Terrorverse, anyway). You? The puny horror movie character? Not so much. There's no clever trap you can set. No magic words that will make him disappear. When Satan says "die," you say "how violently?" It's that easy. Unless you have the balls to stand up to him.

Picture this: You're battling the devil. Maybe he's in human form, or maybe (budget permitting) he's chosen a more traditional representation—a red, fire-breathing goat-demon combo of some kind, each tooth a sharpened gargoyle. His tail whips back and forth, smashing nearby statues to pieces. His horns belch black smoke as he saunters toward you. You flatten your back against the cold stone of the exhibit hall, cornered, trying not to stare into those eyes—those dead, sulfur-yellow eyes. This is it. This is how I die. No awkward product placement or jarringly good dialogue can save you now.

He leans in and opens his jaws—the heat coming off his skin blisters

your forehead. His breath takes years off your life (irrelevant, since you're about to die anyway).

And then you remember. There is one thing that can drive the devil away.

SHOW HIM YOUR PENIS. When the devil has you at claw's length, you need something shocking. Something dramatic. Something that will make the entire Terrorverse collapse in on itself. And there's only one object with that much power:

A penis.

I offer this simple equation: Full-frontal male nudity (P) does not exist in the Terrorverse (T). Therefore, if P is present, T cannot be present. And if T is present, P cannot be present.

In other words, if a man lets it all hang out for the world (i.e., the audience) to see, whatever movie he's in cannot, according to the laws of movie physics, be in the horror genre.

If you have a penis? Marvelous. Drop your shorts and make Papa proud.

If you don't? Find someone who does, and fast.

It may seem like a juvenile response to a desperate situation. A sad attempt to mask fear with immature humor. Maybe it is. But would you rather die with dignity or live with nudity?

Are you not—despite everything you've been through—still alive after all these pages? Put your faith in this last step, too. If you're ever face-to-face with Satan, show him the goods.

APPENDIX

ADDITIONAL STUDY MATERIALS

If you want to become a writer, you start by reading the classics. If you want to survive a horror movie, you learn from the characters who've survived the classics (or at least made it to the third act). Your movie collection is a weapon. Load it with the best ammo available.

ALIEN (1979)
Perfection.

ALTERED STATES (1980)
Written by three-time Oscar winner Paddy Chayefsky, this trippy sci-fi horror classic paved the way for later reality-bending films like *Flatliners* and *Jacob's Ladder*.

AN AMERICAN WEREWOLF IN LONDON (1981)
Funny. Scary. Sexy. Hairy.

THE AMITYVILLE HORROR (1979)
My favorite version of that tried-and-true horror conceit: Bad things happen in house. Family buys house. Bad things happen to family. Also, no man's hair has ever looked better than James Brolin's hair in this movie. Trust me. It's worth watching this movie for the hair alone.

THE BABADOOK (2014)
Ba-BA-ba DOOK! DOOK! DOOK!

BLACK CHRISTMAS (1974)
Fun fact: director Bob Clark later directed *A Christmas Story*, thereby creating the greatest Christmas-themed double feature of all time.

THE BLAIR WITCH PROJECT (1999)
The idea everybody wishes they'd thought of first, and the film that launched a thousand found-footage movies.

BRIDE OF CHUCKY (1998)
A deliciously insane series at its deliciously insane best.

THE BURNING (1981)
One of the better *Friday the 13th* knockoffs; the scariest thing about it might be the fact that it was cowritten by Harvey Weinstein.

THE CABIN IN THE WOODS (2012)
A brilliant dissection of the genre, and the reason there will never be a movie adaptation of the book you're currently reading.

CARRIE (1976)
If you haven't seen this masterpiece yet, go to your prayer closet.

CHILDREN OF THE CORN (1984)
A thoroughly creepy take on religious fanaticism and demonic agriculture. And a fun watch, despite some dated special effects.

CHRISTINE (1983)
The reigning champ of the ultrarare evil car genre.

THE CONJURING (2013)
Few people are better at creating tension and crafting scares than James Wan, and his powers are on full display here. One of the best haunted house movies ever made.

CREEPSHOW (1982)
Stephen King playing a hillbilly. Ed Harris disco dancing. E. G. Marshall puking cockroaches. What more do you want?

DAWN OF THE DEAD (1978)
What has a more painful bite, the zombies or the social commentary? George A. Romero skewers American consumerism (and several

characters) in this scary, funny, gory, satirical, sort-of sequel to *Night of the Living Dead*.

DEAD ALIVE (ORIGINALLY RELEASED AS BRAINDEAD) (1992)
The last (and best) of Peter Jackson's early, irreverent, hilarious, low-budget gore-fests. It might be the bloodiest movie of all time.

THE DESCENT (2005)
Neil Marshall's all-female excursion into a creepy cave full of cannibalistic crawlers trades traditional jump scares in favor of a slow build. A deliciously brutal and unforgiving movie.

THE EVIL DEAD 2: DEAD BY DAWN (1987)
The first *Evil Dead* was a wildly original horror movie that introduced horror fans to Sam Raimi and Bruce Campbell. This sequel is even better.

THE EXORCIST (1973)
The power of Christ compels me to watch it at least once a year.

THE FLY (1986)
David Cronenberg's dark portrait of a man falling apart (in every sense), loosely based on the 1958 original. The role Jeff Goldblum was born to play, if you believe in that sort of thing.

THE FOG (1980)
A good old-fashioned atmospheric ghost story—slowly, creepily building to an unforgettable climax.

FRIDAY THE 13TH (1980)
The movie that invented half the rules this book teaches.

GET OUT (2017)
If you're a filmmaker, this is one of those movies that makes you want to crawl under a rock and die because you'll never make anything as good, and Jordan Peele did it on his first attempt.

HALLOWEEN (1978)

The movie that invented the other half—and made John Carpenter an instant legend. Yes, the 2018 reboot is good, but if you haven't seen either, start with the original.

HEREDITARY (2018)

Ari Aster infuses a story of grief and trauma with striking visuals, superior performances, and a jaw-dropping ending—plus a staggering number of beheadings.

THE HILLS HAVE EYES (1977)

You know the old story: Family's car breaks down in the middle of nowhere, family gets attacked by inbred cannibals, family exacts brutal revenge on said cannibals.

HOSTEL (2005)

The first forty minutes are a porno. The next fifty are a series of snuff films. Is this really horror? All I know is I can't stop watching.

HOUSE OF 1000 CORPSES (2003)

Start with one pound of *The Hills Have Eyes*, add a cup of Rob Zombie's insanity-laced blood, and cook over the flames of hell for eighty-nine minutes.

INVASION OF THE BODY SNATCHERS (1978)

A bug-eyed Donald Sutherland, a pre-*Fly* Jeff Goldblum, and Mr. Spock (sans ears). Directed by Philip Kaufman before his Oscar-nominated career took off.

IT (2017)

The biggest horror movie of all time, and one of the best. As a producer for the film I'm biased, but Andy Muschietti made a classic.

IT FOLLOWS (2014)

A love letter to horror movies that is a great horror movie in its own right.

JAWS (1975)
Young, hungry Spielberg. Young, hungry shark. Perfect script. Perfect cast. You're gonna need a bigger boat.

LAST HOUSE ON THE LEFT (1972)
Another well-worn tale: Psychos rape and murder girls. Psychos move in with one of the girls' parents. Parents bite off psycho's penis.

THE LOST BOYS (1987)
This movie has it all: A gang of hard-partying California vampires riding dirt bikes (and eating Chinese food, for some reason), the Coreys at their peak, death by antler, and—yes—shirtless saxophone solos. Who says you can't be dead *and* sexy?

MISERY (1990)
Rob Reiner bats .1000 when it comes to Stephen King adaptations.

NIGHT OF THE LIVING DEAD (1968)
The one and only.

A NIGHTMARE ON ELM STREET (1984)
Wes Craven creates a new species of slasher, and Johnny Depp gives the phrase "wet the bed" a new meaning.

THE OMEN (1976)
Think of this film as the final installment in a satanic trilogy beginning with *Rosemary's Baby* and *The Exorcist*. All three feature superior scripts, actors, and directors, and all three have that tasty grittiness of the mid-'60s to late '70s.

THE OTHERS (2001)
A stylish, subdued take on the classic haunted house movie. Nicole Kidman crushes.

PARANORMAL ACTIVITY (2007)
Oren Peli wrote, produced, directed, shot, and edited the original version of this movie in *seven days*. In other words, he could've watched

the tape from *The Ring* and still created a horror franchise before Samara came out of the TV to kill him.

PET SEMATARY (1989)
The movie that crosses a sacred line, turns around, pisses on that line, and goes on its merry way.

PHANTASM (1979)
Unlike other super-low-budget late-'70s horror directors, Don Coscarelli wasn't content with knife-wielding maniacs or summer camps. He was more interested in interdimensional grave robbers and chrome spheres of death.

POLTERGEIST (1982)
Tobe Hooper may have directed it, but this is the most "Spielbergian" horror movie ever made. Jerry Goldsmith's score is unreal.

PSYCHO (1960)
The first (and, for my money, still the best) slasher movie.

THE PURGE (2013)
Is it horror? Maybe. Is it social commentary? Sure. Is it bananas? YES.

A QUIET PLACE (2018)
An imaginative, highly effective (and, frankly, emotionally draining) movie. Between this and *Bird Box*, 2018 was a banner year for postapocalyptic sensory-deprivation horror.

THE RETURN OF THE LIVING DEAD (1985)
A hilarious send-up of the Romero zombie universe—and surprisingly ahead of its time (see: running zombies, talking zombies, even contraption-building zombies). Fast, disgusting, and overflowing with nudity. Written and directed by Dan O'Bannon, cowriter of *Alien*.

THE RING (2002)
Perhaps the best American remake of an Asian horror film, with the most terrifying opening sequence since *Pee-Wee's Big Adventure*.

ROSEMARY'S BABY (1968)

One of the scariest movies of all time, without an ounce of gore. Any film that can make Scrabble scary is an automatic masterpiece.

SAW (2004)

James Wan's directing debut spawned a host of imitators and a million sequels, but none lived up to this film's superior performances or monster twist.

SCANNERS (1981)

Another David Cronenberg study of humans playing god with science—this time to gain telepathic powers. You're probably wondering, "Do we get to see a head explode in this movie?" The answer is yes. Yes, we do.

SCREAM (1996)

In which Wes Craven simultaneously makes an insanely good horror movie and subverts some of the very horror tropes he helped create.

SE7EN (1995)

I went to see this film by myself on a cold, rainy Boston day. I haven't smiled since.

THE SHINING (1980)

The best movie ever made? Or merely the best horror movie ever made? A question for the ages.

THE SILENCE OF THE LAMBS (1991)

Can you name another horror movie that won an Oscar for Best Picture?

THE SIXTH SENSE (1999)

The movie that made Shyamalan a verb.

SLEEPAWAY CAMP (1983)

The most insane final minute in the history of cinema.

SLUMBER PARTY MASSACRE (1982)
Take some busty teenaged girls, add an escaped mental patient, and you've got the romantic comedy hit of the summer! Just kidding. He kills them all.

THE STEPFATHER (1987)
Terry O'Quinn's seemingly normal (yet quietly psychotic) parent is up there with Jack Nicholson's Jack Torrance in *The Shining*. A vastly underrated movie.

SUSPIRIA (1977)
Italian master Dario Argento's flamboyant, inventive, acid-trippingly colorful opus is one of the best-looking horror movies of all time. Luca Guadagnino's 2018 remake takes a more muted, grounded approach but is an effective film in its own right.

THE TEXAS CHAINSAW MASSACRE (1974)
It's all right there in the title.

THE THING (1982)
John Carpenter and Kurt Russell at their tough-as-nails, hard-drinking, unshaven best. Never mind the comparisons to *Alien*. Never mind the fact that it bombed. It's a must-see. Dog lovers be warned.

28 DAYS LATER (2002)
OK, so not all zombies are laughably slow and clumsy. Or (technically speaking) zombies.

THE WITCH (2015)
Maybe the most restrained film on this list, this stretches the definitions of what a horror movie can be. Robert Eggers creates a wholly original, exquisitely detailed portrait of a family in 1630s New England filled with atmospheric dread that slowly builds to a hypnotic finale.

ACKNOWLEDGMENTS

Thanks to all my friends at Quirk, especially: Doogie "The Doogieman" Horner, Melissa "Depths of Hell-O" Monachello, and David "Put the Lotion in the Basket" Borgenicht. A special rattle of the bones goes to Jason "Invaders from the Planet" Rekulak, who's guided me through three books now, despite the fact that we've never met. The way I see it, this means (A) he's a ghost who needs to nurture one last writer before he can find eternal peace, (B) I'm insane, and he only exists in my imagination, or (C) we do everything by e-mail.

I wouldn't have survived without my beloved "Monster Squad," a group of grown men who've retained a sad (for them) but helpful (to me) adolescent passion for horror movies. Jason "Dug Grave" Dugre, Steve "To Hell I Go" Sabellico, Brent "The Nice Guy with the Monosyllabic First Name" Simons, and Eric "The Nebbish Jew" Goldman—along with member at large Kevin "Ch-Ch-Ch" Chesley.

Finally, a special thanks to Cody Zwieg—and an extra-special thanks to Wes Craven.